The HAL Philosophy

- The Next Steps of the Progression Work

Randi Green

The HAL Philosophy

- The Next Steps of the Progression Work

The HAL Philosophy
- The Next Steps of the Progression Work

Copyright © 2020 Randi Green
Publisher: BoD – Books on Demand, Copenhagen, Denmark
Print: BoD – Books on Demand, Norderstedt, Germany

Layout: Randi Green
ISBN 978-87-430154-5-1
97887 43015451
2nd Edition

Website
www.toveje.dk
Higher Awareness Lifestyle

Other Books from the same Author
The Souls of Humanity
Terralogy
Understanding the Old Stellar Souls
Reconstruction of the Planetary Soul
Modern History

Table of Contents

A New Way of Learning 7

What is the HAL Philosophy? 10

The HAL Material So Far 16

On the HAL Progression Work 17

The HAL Project 23

Why Do the HAL Progression Work? 26

On the Progressive Systems 30

The New Grand Cycle 37

The 6 Developmental Realities 42

The Unfolding of the NGC into Our System 51

The Emplacement in 2020-2021 59

The 5 Human Reality Zones 62

The Solar System Nations 65

Template Work & The First Two Pillars 75

Reality Governance & The Third Pillar 84

Relative Reality & Segregation Dynamics 87

The Challenges of the Councils 91

The Bad Choices of the Minority 97

The Big Choices 112

The Individual Challenges 115

The Reality Jurisdictions 130

The Old Racial Contracts 148

The Prohibiting Technologies 161

The Difficulty of Our System 170

The Rehabilitation Zone 172

How to Use the HAL Books 178

Letting Go of Outdated Beliefs 181
The Meaning of I...191
Processing Information..193
Creating Higher Order Ideas 200
New Adjustable Paradigms..206
The Expanded Human 210
Developing Our Higher Order Senses......................................215
Energy, Consciousness and Life...219
On Order, Balance and Harmony 224
On the Progression Rate..233
What is a Principle, Rule or a Law?..237
On the 12 Principles of Progression 238
On the 12 Rules of Engagement...244
The 12 Choices of Living 247
The 12 Natural Laws of Energy Utilization 248
For the 2nd Edition 249
On the Upgrade of the Universes...251
On the Changes in the Sun 255
The Three Levels of Energies 259

A New Way of Learning

Before we go deeper into the material, creating the foundation for the HAL Philosophy paradigm and line of thought, let us contemplate a bit on how to process the information, I give.

Becoming an Active Reader
Now, when working with the HAL material, you are to learn new ways of processing information and concepts. You must educate yourself to be able to process the higher order information, I share with you.

Therefore, if you get frustrated with the information, just think about it as an expansion of your brain capacity and that upgrading it takes time. Your brain capacity has been downsized and working with my information is like building a lot of new synaptic patterns into the brain. Consequently, I am not just trying to make you work with and grasp new concepts; I am attempting to advance your brain into new heights. So, be patient with yourself and work with the material many times. Work with it until you can read, process and understand it with no difficulties. As long as you struggle, there is additional capacity to be built in.

Thus; the HAL material is a new line of thought and a new way of processing information. You have to develop your brain to be able to work with the material, because the ways I present it are new to you, compared to the ways of working with information as you are used to. I do not present the information in a linear way. I present the information in patterns, with repetitions, and within the context it belongs. As an example, if I write about some higher order concepts, I might add in a memory or some higher order information that fits the metaphysical explanation. Makes it practical or relevant. I might jump between layers of information, using the different levels of energy, which are needed to build the correct understanding of the ideas, I want to share with you. I also work with the same ideas in different ways.

This means that the information is given in frames of ideas within frames of ideas – spaces within spaces. On top of that, I might refer to previously written concepts from my other books. Not explaining it again. So; you are to sharpen up, remembering the information – or write it down and become an active reader. Have the books at your disposal, so you can look up the references to concepts etc.

Why Do it This Way?
I do it this way, because I am trying to build the new energetic mind-patterns, you need to be able to conceptualize the new ideas.

As far as we know, everything in nature is built upon geometrical patterns. The brain's synapses work in a similar way. The brain cells and synapses work in groups of neurons capable to process identical energies. That is, they fire in energetic clusters and because of that, the traditional teaching techniques are counterproductive. The linear teaching technique is in opposition to the energetic patterns found in all information and how systems of information are built.

That is the first new way for you to learn to process information, i.e. that all information is energy constructing a pattern, and you are to learn how to connect all the dots in the pattern. You are also to learn how to work with the tiny glimpses of visual information, you see in your inner perception field, to be able to decode the energetic patterns you are presented to either in my work or in your own inner work. With the latter, I allude to the common mistake of approaching the inner visual and auditory information from a linear viewpoint. If you do it that way, you are bound to miss the patterns of the higher order information systems, they are part of.

Therefore, all information you get - be it only a tiny glimpse - will always be part of a larger pattern, expanding into higher and higher levels of energy from *the rings of progression*, our world is built upon. Regrettably for now, the rings of progression are highly distorted and therefore, the importance of the personal clearing and timeline work, I advocate for, to enable us to work our way back into all that we are.

Additionally

1) A good idea is to take notes when I present a concept, an idea or create a new word. I will probably use abbreviations and if I do, the first time I write the word, I write it in full and then in brackets, I write the abbreviation. An example could be the Interactive Simulation Program (the ISP). There is no real list of abbreviations – you do that on a piece of paper or in your notebook - and then you can look it up, if you forget what the shortenings mean. Write it down or just the page number, so you can find it again and read it.

2) Also write down the definitions in your notebook that are in my books. Including the page number, so you can look them up again.

When writing the information down, the brain-hand connection generates a stronger energy pattern in your brain, since you are expressing your thoughts onto paper and from the "inside" and out into your reality. And no notes on the computer – onto paper and into the real world. Not just into the virtual world that has been created with the Internet. We need things to manifest in the matter world and not just in the virtual, holographic world, the Internet is.

What is the HAL Philosophy?

To be able to generate new ways of being human, we need many new paradigms. We need upgraded versions of anatomy, of psychology and pioneering ways of perceiving the nature of reality.

Generally speaking, we need new frames of reference into which we can conceptualize our lives, who we think we are, what we want to become, and how we perceive our surroundings. All of this, and more, is what I am working with and to create a framework for my material, the best approach is to call it a philosophy.

A philosophy is, if you look it up in the google dictionary
1) A theory that acts as a guiding principle for behavior.
2) The study of the essential nature of knowledge, reality and existence.

All of that encompasses how I work. The HAL material follows the old guidelines of philosophy, where I work with the nature of things and try to understand how reality is built, using observation and thinking, instead of computers and mathematics. Thus, the general name for the HAL material is the HAL Philosophy.

The HAL Philosophy investigates human behavior, ethics and the expanded human capacity to progress into a sentient being, living by the accord of the highest principles and progression possibilities our world offers to balance out confusion and chaos. It is a new way of perceiving the nature of things, reality, energy and consciousness.

Philosophers contemplate on how everything is built, made and created and for what purpose. Science observe, define and reduce to be able to produce valid evidence for their ideas. I cannot claim any scientific evidence of my work. Thus, it has to be a philosophy; a way of perceiving life, so that you can choose new ways of being you and what behavior, you want to develop, by utilizing the ideas I offer of what it means to be human in this reality.

The Roots

The HAL Philosophy has roots in mainstream psychology, economics, politics, ethics and science, and it combines and elevates these basic concepts into a higher order approach and system of thought – the expanded version of our lower order reality – in new profound ways to systemize what it means to be human, working under an alternate worldview governed by the Principles, the Rules and Energetic Laws. All of which generates a dissimilar foundation of the outer and inner worlds compared to what is commonly accepted by the mainstream society. *The Rules of Engagement* teach us how to be around other humans (and races from other worlds) and how to attain the highest energetic standards. *The Principles* govern the self-initiated and self-chosen progression of consciousness, and *the Laws* teach us how to utilize the energies of the reality, we are part of.

The HAL Philosophy works with two levels of world perception:

The Lower Order Reality

Contemporary sciences, ideas, etc., perceived, defined and clarified by the human lower order faculties of mind.

The Higher Order Reality

Extraordinary sciences and ideas, which used to be unfolded by the advanced human races, in our solar system, of which we are the lower order manifestation.

The HAL Philosophy approaches all the contemporary knowledge and everyday information in a different way, because that is where most begin their journey towards the higher order sciences. Thus, my aim is not to add more distortion to the existing systems of thought, but to clear out the clutter of the lower order systems of thought and recreate the higher order systems. It is also an attempt to provide a new set of ideas of how we can interpret human history, the artifacts, and relics etc. found in archaeological excavations. The way findings have been defined so far has been from a slightly biased point of view and because of that, human history has been kept at a halt.

The Premise
The premise of the HAL Philosophy is that contemporary humans are the ancestors of extremely advanced human civilizations, which once inhabited our solar system. We find traces of the original solar system civilizations all over the world in cultural mythology, religions, occult teaching systems, sciences and in the soil. It is also lodged into the human genome as cellular memories and hidden in our subconscious mind as part of what C.G. Jung called the Collective Unconscious, although these levels are highly distorted due to the wrongful usage of energy and because of that, disconnecting us from the memories of our planetary race. Additionally, we also suffer from the effects of the reengineered advanced technologies, which once were used by our ancestors in productive ways but later took part in the hijacking of our solar system and the demise of our race. The hijacking did not happen out of the blue – our ancestors laid the possibility for that in their choices and experimentation with our solar system.

Therefore, my progression work - on this timeline - is an attempt to generate a paradigm of what it means to be the human ancestors of these advanced races, as well as how to foresee and meet up with the incoming energies from the new grand cycle and the many waves of changes following from this. However, since most of the advanced technologies are in the progressive higher order levels of our reality, we cannot access these as we are at this time, but we can begin the restoration of what we are by doing the timeline and template work, and make a willed and deliberate effort to get back to what we once were, with the capacity we have now. We are to become once more, but within this reality and in ways that will allow for an adaptation to whatever might come our way.

The premise is – listed up for further contemplation

1) The original solar system humans (also called true humans to differ from the downsized earth human, we are today) was an extremely advanced race that had a highly evolved capacity, which allowed them to work directly with all forms of energy. Technologies were developed, but in ways we are far from understanding, since they were made of mixtures of energy and consciousness.

2) Due to wrongful use of the advanced technologies and wars among the true human races and the otherworldly regressed races, the true human civilizations underwent a full transition from higher order worlds into lower order worlds.

3) The human DNA, cells and lower order energy fields still hold the memory imprints of these civilizations. We can find traces of our ancestry in the collective unconscious, on the microbial levels and in the soil.

4) The technologies, we used to administer, still exist in higher systemic versions of our reality, i.e. on the higher order levels and other energy bands of reality, our planet also holds.

5) Earth humans are bound to repeat, or play out, their hidden history in different setups until they remember and begin to restore their genetics to hold their true purpose and heritage.

13

Lots to Be Uncovered

When that is said, there is a lot to be uncovered to get to the original versions of our ancestry and history. Science has a long way to go, and so have we, to uncover the truth about our ancestry and what we truly are. Information has been kept from us or twisted into inexact history, only holding small bits of the truth of what we are. Or, even worse, directly giving misleading information to hide the true nature of our reality and what humans are capable of in their true form.

Disclaimer

In all my material, and in the here presented HAL Philosophy, I work with what I can remember of the higher order sciences, knowledge and information. What I share is not a matter of right or wrong, but of adding new levels of complexity to contemporary information and to pull forth more details of the true progressive worlds, we are part of.

The truth about our reality is unimaginably for most, since only a few humans hold the amount of consciousness needed to truly get the higher order technologies and how they work.

If we try to grasp the higher order levels of knowledge with the current human mind, we are bound to fail. The brain must be trained to be able to function in the higher order energies and understand the higher order information structures.

I do not claim, what I know, to be science or the ultimate truth. It is what I have experienced, observed and from that I have deduced my assumptions, according to the brain capacity I had at the time and the abilities, I had developed to read the information in the different timelines, just like anybody else working with energetic information and the nature of things.

The way I gain information is not through channeling. It stems from the timeline work and the reading of the information I get on the timelines. If there is communication with other density humans or regressed races, it is through a direct encounter energetically, visually and auditory using my energy fields as the place for this arrangement in the other dimensions. Every piece of information, I receive, I exam through the looking-glass of the higher order scientific knowledge to eliminate any distortion and subconscious material. Naturally, if this appears, I clear it out to reach the accurate level of information.

Always remember; what we see and understand fits our current brain capacity and what our lower order fields hold of distortions. The more distortion, our lower order fields hold, the more difficult it is to perceive beyond the deception programs and derail mechanisms of our reality. Hence, the closer the brain operates to the base program level, the less valid the information becomes. However, the higher up we go in energy, the more correct the information will be, but *only* if the ones decoding the information of the observed are equipped to do so, and *only* if the ones decoding the information have developed the mandatory higher order reading and sensing faculties and know how to use the higher order processing abilities to discern between the lower order distortions and the correct information of the past, present and future hidden in our timelines. And of course, knows how to work beyond the prohibiting technologies.

The reason why humanity has not cracked the case of operating at their complete capacity is simple. Humanity has forgotten how to progress and develop themselves into the higher order version, they could be and used to be. Let us change that.

Notice these abbreviations for future references
Before the timeline event (BTE)
Under the timeline event (UTE)
After the timeline event (ATE)
The Less Progressive Universe (the LPU)
The New Grand Cycle (the NGC)

The HAL Material So Far

If you are new to the ideas of the Higher Awareness Lifestyle (called HAL for short), I suggest you read all my 2014-2017 books, such as *the Souls of Humanity* and *Modern History*. *Terralogy* is also a good read to understand how the humanoid regressed genetics work in humans, and *Understanding the Old Stellar Souls* is a fine supplement to grasp some of the restrictions, which have been put onto our higher order energy system as the end result of the hijacking of our solar system.

I have a lot of free material on the Internet, so you can get more concepts there. Of course, I can only advice you to do my HAL Classes & Courses get the understandings taught in the HAL Basic Class, the HAL Advanced Classes 1-4, the HAL Completed Classes 1-2 and the Future Human Project Courses 1-4. The HAL Classes & Courses deliver the 2017-2019 concepts and information.

My focus is to educate people to be able to process the higher order levels of information and to make anyone who is eager to do so, ready to think in more progressive ways. Because, as the mind expands so does the ability to adapt to changes along with the knowledge of how to face the changes, and what they bring about, in productive ways.

My work is also about what we can change into, if we are willing to do the needed work of clearing and transformation. But most of all, my work is about changing our world into what it was supposed to be at this time and in this universe. The latter is part of the transition work.

So, let us begin.

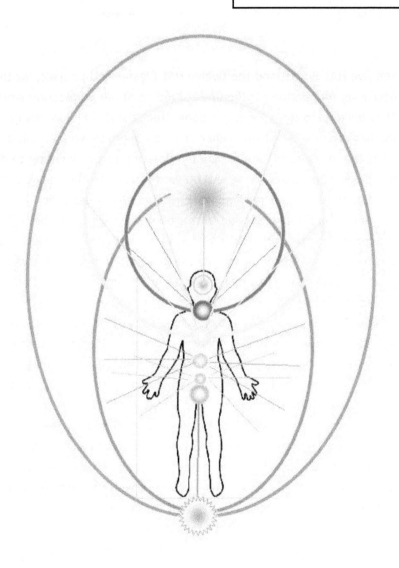

On the HAL Progression Work

The five HAL Books, and the twelve HAL Classes and Courses, lay the necessary foundation for the understanding of *the progression work*. They build up to the level in this book. Thus, the HAL Philosophy gives the last pieces of what the higher order progression work entails and what the implications are for contemporary humans, wanting to do the progression work today and onward. And from there, hopefully wanting to begin *the transition work* into the new grand cycle.

Hence, in the first section of this book we begin with the higher order levels of the progression work and the last bits of the work that can be taught. The idea is to give the information needed to set the goals of what we are to strive for, and why it is important for us to do so. From this level of understanding, it will be easier to make effective choices of what to do, and how. At least then, whatever is chosen, will be from a level of understanding and then it can finally be said – at the end of this cycle - that humans had a chance to exercise their free will to choose, whether or not they wanted to do the transition work to match the requirements of the new grand cycle.

Free will only applies, if the ones exercising it know the costs of the choices, they are to choose between – on an educated level – as in what each choice has of implications in this and the following lives, because every choice done in any lifetime affects our chiasm and our progression rate, as in what section of the progression spiral we are emplaced into, the next time we take on an organic vessel within this system. All choices done in a lifetime set the tone of the energies we must transform and work with, in the next life, as part of the attained energy system as well as what type of consciousness, we will get. And of course, then what type of organic vessel, we can expect from that. None of these understandings are new, however the HAL Philosophy is lodged into a dissimilar context compared to that of the many other teaching systems given to humanity over the ages regarding the ideas of continued existence in other dimensions.

The HAL Philosophy is not in any ways or forms, a continuation of any preceding philosophical, spiritual or religious systems. In most cases the HAL Philosophy disregards these systems.

But the essence in the ideas of moral and ethics are similar to that of other teaching systems, since all information given to humanity stem from the same concepts of the most optimal inter-relational human behavior that stretches back to the original humanities living in our solar system and how they arranged their civilizations, living amongst other human races and humanoid species to ensure common grounds.

Conversely, the HAL Philosophy is not just about inter-human relations or about humans living in an isolated environment as the only living species in our system, but about how humans are to behave in a solar system inhabited by other-dimensional humanities and humanoids as well as being energetically connected to worlds beyond contemporary human understanding.

Therefore, the HAL Philosophy and the HAL Progression Work diverge from other, or similar, teaching systems due to the other-dimensional understanding, what a human is and how we can choose to progress all that we are, on an energetic level and on a consciousness level.

What is also to be noticed, is that the HAL Philosophy does not include any divine powers or godly creators in any ways or forms. Most of the old systems involve a cosmos founded by deities or a singular deity, from which humans are a creation to serve some sort of function of these creators. In fact, none of the old teaching systems incorporate a scientific conceptualization of higher order realities unfolded within a vast range of universes inhabited by other human civilizations. On the contrary.

The HAL Philosophy approaches all ancient ideologies as constructions made by other-reality human races, living in adjacent worlds vibrating energetically unalike our world, or humanoid species having produced similar teaching systems as the means of control of humanity.

Because of this, the HAL Philosophy explanations, ideas and concepts, of why humanity should embark on a willed progression journey, are vastly different from that of other teaching systems.

And, what also differs, in the HAL attempt to remind humanity of their eternal and true power, is the new grand cycle (the NGC) knocking at our door and the rolling completion of the old cycles that is happening now and has been unfolding for the last 2550 years. Because of the NGC, all choices made in this lifetime will determine if we get a chance to continue an existence within the future universes that arise from the makeover done by the new grand cycle.

The Chiasm
The chiasm – as explained in the prior HAL material – is our individual timeline map and it carries the recordings of the timelines, we have participated in. The chiasm holds the energetic and genetic end-result of how we have utilized our consciousness units in the template and in our energy system, in this and all lifetimes. What is recorded into the chiasm determines the possible futures, we can expect.

The Timeline and Clearing Work empower us and give us the abilities to adjust our present circumstances by transforming the energies and genetics of the past, using the holographic projection mechanism of the chiasm. It is up to us to choose to clear our template and what it holds of energies and genetics stuck on timelines in long-gone worlds within unfinished play outs, not cleared properly when we lived that life, or undetected alternate possible timelines created by the choices we made and the ways, we chose to express our potentials in these worlds.

The Essence of the HAL Progression Work

Progression is about taking full responsibility for all that we are and change what does not work, relative to what we want to become. It is also about facing the challenges of our lives, in this world, to get to where we are supposed to be and in that, reunite with the energetic standards and progression rate of our system.

The life we have, and our surroundings, show us where we are on the progression spiral and what we need to clear to gain the highest purity rate by unfolding the highest standards in what we exemplify, what we create and what we are. We do that to achieve the highest progression rate, which ensures an emplacement on the progression spiral according to our deeds, actions and achievements.

The inner and outer progression work focus on what is attainable and achievable to guarantee a better emplacement in the upcoming rounds of existence as well as the work to upgrade our current energy system and template, which will secure an even better emplacement in the next rounds, if we do both.

The HAL Progression Work is thus about making the ideal choices, following the guidelines of *the Principles of Progression.* It is about the ways we behave around other lifeforms, and how to obtain the highest standards by exercising *the Rules of Engagement* and finally the HAL Progression Work is about how we administer *the Natural Laws of Energetic Utilization* in our creations and manifestations of any form of energy. All sections are needed to reach the highest goals of progression.

To Summarize

1) *The HAL Philosophy* provides ideas of how to live a human life unfolding and living by the higher order awareness, all aimed at reuniting consciously with the progressive worlds and their advanced human civilizations.

2) *The HAL Progression Work* focus on the ethical and energetic behaviors we have, as contemporary humans in this world, to become the best version of a human we can be. It also entails the work of preparing our energy system and consciousness units for continued existence. The Principles of Progression, the Rules of Engagement and the Natural Laws of Energetic Utilization are our guidelines in this.

3) *The Timeline and Clearing Work* transform our energy system, template and the consciousness genetics. *The contemporary goal* is to upgrade these levels by achieving the highest purity rate on the bio-organic level in the ways we live, the highest standards on the energetic level in the ways we behave and the highest progression rate on the consciousness level. *The future goal* of our work is to match the requirements of the NGC. We do that by clearing out all disruptive timelines and our participation in these, as well as all dysfunctional energies and infected consciousness units.

The HAL Project

Our world is bigger than we think and we need to incorporate that into our world perception to truly grasp the higher order sciences such as the understanding of our reality field, as well as the energetic laws governing us and our world, unfolding the full version of our reality. If we continue to exclude these levels of our reality from our perception and understanding of our solar system, we will exclude our chances of new perspectives, alternatives and solutions to a better future for us all. The contemporary human perception will not give us the needed solutions to the transition challenges, we are to face in the upcoming years within all levels of society.

Solutions to generate the higher order sciences, in order to solve the health issues, climate changes, environmental challenges along with the transition challenges, which will follow the new grand cycle, within all areas of human systems and structures. The years to come will alter all aspects of what it means to be human in this world.

The Changes to Come

Humanity are to adapt to the energetic changes and learn to live in energetic flux as the other dimensions become an integral part of our perception of reality. We are also to learn to administer the effects of the past, the present and the future in our daily efforts to follow the Principles, Laws and Rules, which originally governed our world. As the timeline event subsides, humanity – as part of this solar system – will return to the original progressive ways of our reality. Humanity has to develop a new awareness based upon an interactive reality, with new sciences, with new concepts of energy and matter, and the awareness of higher order consciousness. With the higher awareness lifestyle, changes are bound to unfold in the human perception field and develop the psychological faculties, altering what it means to be human. With the HAL Project, we will learn to focus on the world we have vs. the world we want and how to build it using the Principles, the Rules of Engagement and the Natural Laws of Energetic Utilization to do so.

The Vision for a Better Future
The goal of the HAL Project is to inspire and to develop the higher order awareness, into a new human progressive, communicative and positive developmental and environmental awareness, to be able to do creational projects or create new business projects to manifest the possible highest order reality into our world, for the highest good of the many.

The How
1) The offered possibility to do the true human transition by changing the bio-field, the emotional and mental fields into the higher order energy system, composed of the vibration and the radiation fields.

2) Developing new forms of energy work to reconnect to the original progressive ways, using the Principles, the Rules of Engagement and the Natural Laws of Energy Utilization.

3) Developing creational projects and small businesses where the HAL Project can be unfolded into manifested reality with the main goal of generating a higher order society, based upon higher awareness. This includes generating a better environment for the future humanities and their evolutions, expressing this into a purposeful life, while working with consciousness and energy.

The Inner-Outer Human Evolution

1. The understanding of self and our reality must change to be able to follow the incoming energies of the new grand cycle.
2. New perspectives have to be offered so new purposes for the continued evolution of humanity can unfold, into which new business, creational and personal projects take part, together with a future vision from where the strategies can be defined to reach the goals.
3. Productive solutions and adaptable new ways of being human have to be offered, showing humans as part of a higher order human race in a joint evolution towards a new reality, we will build using these new sciences and understandings.

The Inner-Outer Human

A human is the manifested energy shown on three levels:

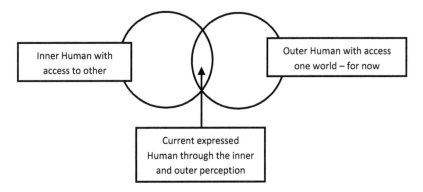

The inner-outer human is an expression of the interaction potentials governed by the Principles, the Rules of Engagement and the Natural Laws of Energetic Utilization. These are the fundamental dynamics that ensure the highest purity rate, the highest standards and the highest progression rate, from which we rebuild our progressive energy system. That is needed for the higher awareness to develop in us.

Why Do the HAL Progression Work?

Today, as I see it, most humans have lost their understanding of what life is about. The true purpose of life, so to speak. For many people, the purpose of life is to build up a family, get a fine career, get lots of money, get a high position in society, have interesting hobbies and be entertained in various forms. That is a valid choice of course, if that is what seems important, but it is not the whole story. And no, the extra we can add to life is not spirituality, religion or any beliefs in a god, or gods, or any forces outside ourselves showing us the inner worlds in an appearance pretending to be guides or angels. These are, in most cases,[1] holographic deception entities found in many of the ancient teaching systems. So, let us dive right into the deep end.

The Basic Steps
The first step in the human awakening process is to accept that reality is more than just the obvious and the tangible. Then, once that is kind of accepted, the next step is the ability to discern between distortion, the derail mechanisms and the holographic deception technologies, and the precise higher order information. Eventually, the ones that are ready can grow into holding the capacities of comprehending and how to work on the other dimensions and densities in the higher and lower order realities, our solar system is part of. Thus, the awakening process is firstly about an acceptance of the unacknowledged hidden realities and then it is about getting back to our true potentials, to be

---

[1] Some of these human hybrids are middle domain avian-mammal humans stemming from 4th dimensional genetic experiments done by the Niburians and the Sirian A infused Arcturians. They are still around along with other hybrid creatures seeded into long-gone worlds, that once existed adjacent to our reality.

able to integrate all that we are as true humans, and then the process must move into a relearning process of what it means to be human on this planet. That is the higher order awareness way of living.

The Opening of the Heart Field

The clearing work is about accomplishing the correct vibration in our heart field to open up into our higher order sensing system. We need that sensing system to be able to work with the hidden worlds. The heart field energizes the mind-field, and change it into the brain-field, which enables us to sense, see and work on the higher order densities and sub-dimensions with the higher order perception faculties.

Consequently, the first step of the clearing work is done with the purpose of clearing out all the distortions lodged into the lower order fields, which restrict all humans from unfolding their potentials. We do that through the proper use of energy on the timelines connected to our energy system, be it in the past, present or future by the use of the Principles, the Rules and the Laws and in the progression work.

Another Type of History

Now, humans on this planet have been through many different stages of advanced existence. It is not as science tells us; i.e. that we were bipedal monkeys grown out of evolutionary processes and now have turned into what we are today.

One group of the hominids were a type of failed experiment from some of the otherworldly races experimenting here and other groups were humans from the colonies that were hit by the contamination – probably due to failed genetic experiments to prolong their lifespan after the timeline event – which led to a complete genetic breakdown and subsequently turned this group into regressed human apes more animal-looking than human-looking. We are correspondingly to grasp that humans in this reality used to be part of a much larger project of transforming energy and consciousness by the use of organic vessels and energetic forms in our system. We chose to do this, to manage and develop our reality from a higher order scientific perspective, in order to progress within the construction of our solar system.

And we are to accept that the human race in its ancient version began an ambitious project a long time ago to secure a continuance of the old warring extra- and intra-systemic races by transforming all that we were into newly created organic vessels with the state of the art holographic code systems and advanced genetic templates above any preceding genetic engineering. And lastly, we seeded these new types of organic vessels into highly organized progressive worlds[2] in this universe and others, within the framework of the very advanced and ancient reality constructions made by the Ancient Ones.[3]

We began this ambitious project by agreeing on specific rules in our interaction with any lifeform in this and other similar worlds. The Principles, the Rules and the Laws were meant to secure peace and non-hostility amongst the races that joined the project, along with being the guidelines on how to progress for the highest good of the many, i.e. for all that joined the project. Here and in all universes.

And we agreed that any encounter between the extra- and intra-systemic human races always should be in the spirit of cooperation and looked-for teamwork with the purpose of achieving the highest order progression for all involved. The highest order progression is to attain the standards of the Ancient Ones.

We set out to progress all that we were and could become along with developing the energetic and technological resources of every

---

[2] We chose the idea of progression contra to the warring realities we had been part of before beginning the project of the 12 human lineages. Most of the 3rd, 4th and 5th cycles of the old worlds collapsed due to wars.

[3] We got the allowances to alter some of the settings of their constructions but only because agreements were made to achieve this. These agreements stated that if we could not complete the project, the constructions would reset to default.

reality into a higher order system, to meet up with the standards of the Ancient Ones. The Ancient Ones were once a highly advanced human race that existed in the very early stages of the evolutionary cycles and had completed these with valor, honor and dignity. The Ancient Ones developed from this group of universes – after having completed the universal level - into other higher order evolutionary cycles of consciousness, where they continued their progression and evolution within realities beyond our current comprehension.

This means, that the awakening process, the clearing work and the progression work is not just about reconnecting to our higher order capacities and activating the correct energy system and template, with what is stored there of memories of other lives in other systems, but also to understand that we are part of a much larger progression journey into several universes, where other human races exist and are doing their version of progressive evolution, i.e. the completed inner and outer human consciousness, mastering energy and consciousness in the reality they are part of.

The HAL Progression Goals
- Educating humans on a psychological level to enable them to develop their consciousness potentials.
- Reaching for the highest energetic, intellectual and emotional performance in life, generating a high-performance culture with progressive attitudes to self, others and our reality.
- Educating humans to create by their own means and by their own resources to develop innovative and inventive projects to support a collective sustainable future.

With that, let us begin the higher order context of the HAL Philosophy.

On the Progressive Systems

In the free worlds, no one is forced to progress if they do not want to. That is a valid choice. Nobody can be urged into progression against their will. They can evolve later, if they choose to do so and return to *the progression path* at any time. If they refuse to progress, they will fall further and further behind until they are out of the progressive worlds. From there and onward, they are on *the path of regression*.

This means that if a race persistently does not want to evolve or progress, it is left behind, as explained in *the Souls of Humanity*. Their choice will be taken care of, in the best way possible, since it is part of the cycle of life. The higher order races have lots of technologies to ensure that the different worlds do not breach the systemic settings of other races and their chosen ways of living.

However, since every individual is the first of many and a race is made up by individuals and their choices, efforts are always made to remind those, who are eager to listen, of the ways to return to the progression path. Conclusively, an individual can choose to progress as the first of many and then that individual will move on, even if its race does not want to progress. Nobody is stuck with their race.

There is at all times free movement among all systems; including in worlds like ours, i.e. in exploitation or hijacked systems.

The Focus of Importance
The focus of importance, to the races in the progressive worlds, is the continuation of the original 12 universal human lineages. The original 12 universal human prototypes, i.e. their genetic composition, their energetic build up and their organic form were granted allowances to

exist within the universal structures build by the Ancient Ones. The blueprints for the original 12 universal human lineages are stored in what is called a Library and each system has its own genetic Library. If the genetic blueprint is lost for a race, that lineage will cease to exist and cannot be seeded again. A race can always be reseeded but if the blueprint is destroyed, all is lost. Consequently, the protection of the Libraries is of uttermost importance to the progressive human races in the universal worlds and the preservation of them supersedes all individual and racial choices.

Secondly, the focus is on maintaining the standards of the reality fields, the 12 human lineages were seeded into and the safeguarding of the local worlds, unfolded within the systemic resonance fields and their holographic grids. These fields and their worlds are lodged into the extremely advanced holographic-technological constructions built by the Ancient Ones.

These constructions and their advanced technologies are the very foundation of the progressive worlds, and they are irreplaceable and cannot be re-made. The density constructions and their technologies are called the Workstations, and the core facilities connect all outer, middle, inner and higher worlds (with their parallel sister worlds), as well as run the energetic and consciousness network of all universal reality fields.

To administer the focus of importance the best way, i.e. for the highest good of the many races in all worlds, different higher order councils were created to ensure the highest progression rate, the best developmental programs and collective actions for the races living in the many universes, housing the progressive systems and worlds.

The consequences of any decision, on the grand scale of things, are consequently seen as a community choice of the joined races, and the precedence these races set for their future lineages by the usage of their consciousness genetics, and how they choose to develop their reality fields and systems. All the systems, the worlds and the reality fields are viewed as one joint unit, where the human races exist to evolve, according to their prototype, purpose and function and from that progress their worlds to the highest standards.

The Rings of Progression
When a race chooses to develop and progress, the goal is to get the participating individuals to evolve in a manner, which will develop *the rings of progression*, a race needs to progress as a unified whole.

The rings of progression run the manifested planes of existence - the resonance fields - and they are constructed to unfold the highest values in the progressive human systems. The values are *the highest purity rate*, *the highest standards* and *the highest progression rate*, all of which are the goals to strive for in all the progressive worlds.

The appropriately attained rings of progression set in motion *the progression spiral*, attaching each system to the core facilities of the higher order races. Following this, *the rays of the central sun* energies and dynamics will unfold into that system. The 12 rays are reflected in the 12 Principles, the 12 Rules and the 12 Energetic Laws.

The progression spiral is connected to the holographic teaching systems, the developmental programs, the joint racial memories and the diverse fields of progression dynamics, which a race develops via the use of energy, consciousness and the active template systems.

Through the developmental work on the progression spiral, each human is to learn the abilities to manifest, develop and progress life, energy and consciousness on the individual level (the 1-7 pillar), on the racial level (the 2-8 pillar), on the reality field level (the 3-9 pillar), the systemic level (the 4-10 pillar), and the holographic-technological level (the 5-11 pillar). The human progression work is completed with the abilities to manifest, develop and progress all forms of life, energy and consciousness on the advanced universal level (the 6-12 pillar), having attained the all-inclusive knowledge of how to build, develop and repair the universal constructions of the Ancient Ones.

The Extinction Protocol
Equally, when a race turns regressive, the progression spiral in such a system will degenerate into *a regression spiral* and eventually detach *the rings of regression* from the core facilities. When this happens, such a system is placed under the extinction protocol and its planes of existence will slowly become bereft of everything, because it does not get infused with new progressive energy from the universal network of energy and consciousness.

Following the extinction protocol, the race and its system will be encouraged to seek ways to reconstruct their system and race, under the supervision of the councils and their representatives. The attempt of reconstruction will be monitored closely to observe changes and if the race can be redeemed, so to speak.

A certain portion of time is given to that, but if the race continues to regress and distorts all energies to an extreme degree and in that way harms the resonance fields, or damage the genetic Library of that reality; then that race is seen a danger to the construction and a full intervention is the next step.

And intervention is not a good thing. There are severe restrictions to an intervention and the result is often a full racial clear out of that system to preserve the construction, since its race has been deemed failed. If a race has been deemed failed, then its technologies, its life forms and all this race has built will undergo the process of deletion and evaporation. All that is preserved are the ones that have a chance of making the shift into the rehabilitation zone, where the durable humans or humanoids of the original lineages with viable genetics, energy systems and showing good will are given a last chance to get themselves back on track.

After the intervention, what has not made it in the rehabilitation zone, will return to the Library until all forms of life are completed, and then the system and its resonance fields will reset to default. After this, a new seeding can occur from the Library.

The Rehabilitation Zone
Just to make it perfectly clear. The ones, be it human or humanoids, that get the chance of rehabilitation are to rebuild an energy system and energy fields around them, using the accurate ways and energies to do so, i.e. living by the Principles, the Rules and the Laws.

Hence, the rehabilitation zone is not something one is chosen to or shifted into automatically – it is something, the individual must build his or her way into. In that way, the individual shows good will. The access is granted when the mandatory rebuilding work has been done by that individual, and the individual can prove that he or she is worthy to continue his or her existence within the progressive worlds, by living a life following the accords of the progressive systems.

The individual is to prove that he or she has the will to accomplish the highest purity rate, the highest standards and attain the highest progression rate of his or her system, and of the progressive worlds. Only then will the individual enter the rehabilitation zone.

It is a clever system to show the individual's abilities to work with energy, and that he or she knows how to honor life despite the failed system, he or she is part of.

And, to shut down all speculations of the rehabilitation zone as something that happens after this life: Entering will happen, while the person is alive. Not after death. The person must live by the accord of the progressive worlds, as if he or she is there already.

Thus, the worthiness is to be proven while existing, showing that it is understood and integrated by rebuilding the energy system and activating the consciousness genetics in the accurate manner.

It is the recognition of the rehabilitation zone and the accepted responsibilities this reality instills in the individual, that will get him or her acknowledged.

The responsibilities are personal, since each human has a unique energy system, differently developed code sheets and a distinctive chiasm. Each human holds unique consciousness genetics that need different challenges to restore and turn progressive again.

What will develop one individual, might not develop another and therefore, it is not a specific teaching system (or rituals) that will get a person there, but the individual's choice to facilitate the Principles, the Rules and the Laws in a progressive lifestyle, to rebuild the energy system and get the genetics to work in an appropriate manner again.

Exploitation of Other Systems
The councils of all higher order progressive human races also work to free hijacked human systems, transformed into exploitation realities as the consequences of the old wars. Our solar system is one of such systems.

Although, it is accepted for races to remain and choose to stay status quo, exploitation of other human races to preserve one lineage – seeing this lineage as more valuable than other races and because of this, are willing to break the Principles of Progression, the Rules of Engagement and the Natural Laws of Energetic Utilization to do so - is not accepted. Exploitation of other living beings to sustain one's own race, is a violation of all manifestations of life. It is a transgression to be met with severe penalty. It is unaccepted and unwarranted, and there are no extenuating circumstances in the eyes of the councils, when a race chooses this way of living, given the fact that any reality systems based upon exploitation and slavery serve no purpose of any future lineages in an orderly and productive manner.

And of course, that is not what the Ancient Ones gave allowances for to unfold in their universes and henceforth, to preserve the rights to remain here, the councils must ensure that exploitation systems do not continue their existence within the universal network.

Consequently, if a race becomes parasitic by choice or manipulation and chooses to exploit other lifeforms to preserve and sustain itself, this race is seen as a failed race, serving no purpose, and the penalty is to be placed under the extinction protocol and segregated from the progressive worlds.

The New Grand Cycle

The next step in our understanding is that the circumstances, we are in today, differ from the conditions in the previous cycles because of the universal changes coming our way over the next 120 years or so.

Changes, which the progressive human races have dealt with and are dealing with as well. Our solar system, and the many races here, are not the only ones to instigate changes in their ways of living.

The reasons for the changes all spring from the culmination of the timeline event, called the completion cycles, and the new grand cycle that is coming in following the completion. A new grand cycle carries different forms of energy, consciousness and progression possibilities.

Under normal circumstances, the old cycles would be allowed to exist along with it. However, this time the new grand cycle (the NGC) will take all the progressive races into the 6-12 pillar and completely phase out the older cycles, along with what they hold of technologies, lifeforms and consciousness. It must be this way, because most of the races - living by the standards of the older cycles - have failed to meet up with the progression rate of their systems along with the violation of every agreements they have made with the councils as part of the experiment of the Less Progressive Universe (the LPU). The genetic lineages of the ancient worlds are like sinking ships, pulling the entire foundation of all universes to its knees. Since the timeline event is ending and the experiment of the LPU has failed, all must change.

Consequently, the new grand cycle will modify the previous forms of universes, reality fields and planes of existence to undo the mess of the older cycles and their regressive failed races. All the races of the original 12 lineages will shift into the new standards of the NGC with the 6th dimension as the lowest standard in the outer worlds and the 12th dimension as the highest standard in the core worlds. The planes of existence will change, along with the phasing out of the disruptive density 1 (the DE1) energies and genetics in the dimensions 1-3 (D1-3), which will cease to exist in all progressive worlds.

What are the Potentials of the NGC?
The incoming higher order energies of the new grand cycle stem from a minor group of progressive humans in the outskirts of the universal schemes, which completed the work of their 6-12 pillars.

These humans are unknown to us today and they took off from our system – and other similar systems – and built a new reality to continue the 6-12 pillar work in secrecy. This move was chosen by a small group of humans across the original 6-12 pillars, unbeknownst to the councils, as the LPU fell into the hands of the regressive. Of course, the take-off made the systems fall into a lower level of their progression spirals, giving the regressed races the upper hand, but it was a necessary to protect the 6-12 pillar consciousness genetics and the continuation of the original 12 human lineages. All probabilities indicated a failure for the human races in the LPU and the move had to be done before the entire 6-12 pillar project fell into peril. Other groups, from the original 6-12 pillars, stayed behind in all systems to ensure there would be 6-12 pillar humans in all outer worlds, capable of receiving and implementing the cyclic standards of the NGC, when the time was up for this to happen.

This group of progressive humans work under the Ancient Ones and do not refer to the councils. Their objective is vastly different than any objectives of any of the old human races. Their focus of importance is the continuation of the original 12 human lineages to become the new Ancient Ones and the universal work that will lead to immortality.

From their joint effort, the 6-12 pillar level of consciousness, energy and life have been firmly implemented into the core facilities, setting the 6-12 purity rate, the 6-12 standards and the 6-12 progression rate for all future human races.

This work supersedes any decisions and solutions from the councils, and if the higher order councils cannot follow up with the transition work the NGC demands, the 6-12 pillar humanities will take over.

This group of progressive humans is generating the foundation of all future human races to continue within the realities of every universe, after the NGC is over. They will transfer back into our system as part of the new seeding of humans around year 2135, allowing for the 12 universal lineages to be restored in our system. The 6th dimensional template and organic vessel will be part of the reseeding, stemming from the storage units in the 6-12 pillars in all systems.

No contemporary humans in our system, with their existing version of templates, consciousness genetics and organic vessels will be able to match the potentials of the NGC, unless they do the needed clearing and transition work. It is so, because the energy systems in humans are either constructed to support the Interactive Simulation Program (the ISP) or unfold as part of the LPU second chance programs. None of these old developmental programs will continue after 2035, since they failed their purpose of restoring the 12 human lineages.

Contrary to all preceding attempts of restoring the original projects, the incoming potentials of the NGC will enable the 12 human lineages to reenter into the universal planes of existence. The goal of the NGC is to continue a progressive existence following the highest standards as part of the worlds, built by the Ancient Ones. The human races in all universes are to become the next generations of the Ancient Ones, knowing how to engineer universes and how to develop the ancient reality constructions. Something we originally strived for, when we entered the 12 universal lineages, and we vowed to do that with our word. *Our word* is the highest code in our core being. *The Vow* and *the Will* are unfolded via the work, we actively participate in to get there. The original construction of our template was made to meet the requirements of this work, i.e. *the mission statement.*

The 3 highest principles in our essence, were created in collaboration with the Ancient Ones:

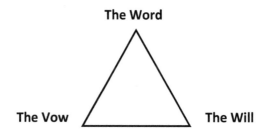

Immortality is one of the benefits of the 6-12 pillar progression work, aside from the skills and abilities to construct and develop universes.

Immortality means to move freely between all worlds and cycles in all systems with a chosen organic vessel of our own construction, and yet remain able to develop into new heights by the progression work, and the integration of the energies and consciousness abilities presented to us in the systems, we choose to take part of. We would not have to shed off our organic form, when shifting between systems, but would be able to develop and upgrade it into whatever is looked-for in the systems, we want to enter and become part of.

On Lemuria and Now

The 6-12 pillar work began in the prior to the timeline event Lemuria on our planet.[4] Historically, it is crucial to understand that our system, and the human races that participated in the Workstations here, were the first to choose the transformation work of changing a system into being able to hold the 6-12 pillar, and hence the complications of the work and destiny of the races here. All races that participated in our system were the forerunners of the new cycle, but failed due to many different circumstances.

And now, the correct level of existence is working its way into our system again. Our solar system is up for the remerging with the 6-12 pillar energies as part of the NGC. That will activate the 6-12 reality grids, we created in the times of Lemuria, and when the high-energy grids run with the 6-12 pillar energies into our planet, the true human energy system will become a possibility for all contemporary humans with viable genetics, dating back to the original 12 human lineages.

For the reason that, as the 6-12 pillar holographic grids ignite in our resonance fields, the original systemic archetypes that are coded into the grids, will activate additionally. From the grid infusions of the highest potentials into our resonance fields, the possibility arises to reunite energetically with what we once were by reconnecting to our racial memories and, following the progression work with the offered potentials, our own memories and potentials are able to return.

In other words: If we have cleared our lower order fields from all distortion and energetic clutter, the original energy system and code sheets attached to our template will spark to life, as the energies of the NGC grow stronger. *Let us go back in time to get why that this.*

---

[4] As mentioned in *the Souls of Humanity*, the perception of movement in space changes according to the density levels of a reality. Thus, there is no time – that is a human construction. And for the record, our planet is not a planet outside the DE1 level, but a multi-dimensional reality field.

The 6 Developmental Realities

Originally, our system was divided into 6 developmental realities with their own versions of progressive humans. Naturally, it is not possible to show an accurate depiction of how our system looked. It can only be a schematic representation. Nevertheless, each reality was set up to accompany the work with energy and the consciousness genetics.

Given that our system was to develop the 6-12 pillar, it was built with 6 developmental realities and their adjacent progression pillars – we can call these towers of other-dimensional existence - into which the races progressed their energetic and consciousness potentials:

1. The 1-7 pillar (the D1-7 individual segment of knowledge).
2. The 2-8 pillar (the D2-8 racial segment of knowledge).
3. The 3-9 pillar (the D3-9 reality field segment of knowledge).
4. The 4-10 pillar (the D4-10 systemic segment of knowledge).
5. The 5-11 pillar (the D5-11 holographic segment of knowledge).
6. The 6-12 pillar (the D6-12 universal segment of knowledge).

The 6 developmental realities held dissimilar versions of the human lineages. These were called *root races*. Each root race had their own variation of energy sequences (what we call DNA) to build the organic vessel, a distinct energy system and specific consciousness units. All the root races were designed to achieve the highest purity rate, the highest standards and the highest progression rate to be met in their realities, assisted by the developmental programs of their pillar and the approved governance of their reality. More on this later on. All had free access to the holographic teaching system and every human knew what direction to go to match the requirements to complete the self-chosen pillar work. These 6 developmental realities and their pillars were connected to the core facilities, aka the Workstations. The primary 5 realities were to be completed in the 6-12 pillar. The 6-12 pillar was constructed as a catch-up pillar of the other 5 pillars and as the humans completed their pillar, they transferred into the 6-12 pillar, where they got new templates, new energy systems and new organic vessels.

And lastly, the 6 developmental realities and their pillars unfolded across 5 domains, composed of density energy and dimensions.

The 5 domains and their planes of existence
- Outer Domain (density 1 – low energy) holds dimension 1-3.
- Middle Domain (density 2 – middle energy) holds dimension 4-6.
- Inner Domain (density 3 – inner energy) holds dimension 7-9.
- Core Domain (density 4 – core energy) holds dimension 10-12.
- Highest Domain (density 5 – highest energy) holds dimension 13-15.

The Progression Spiral is composed of the domains, which constitute the rings of progression

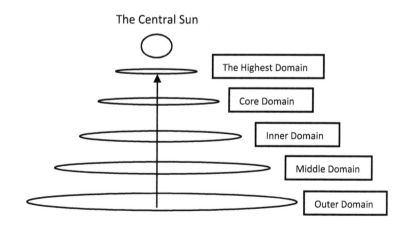

The Central Sun

The Highest Domain

Core Domain

Inner Domain

Middle Domain

Outer Domain

The root races and pillars are positioned in the domains on density 1-5, within 12 dimensions in a ring set up, i.e. *the rings of progression.*

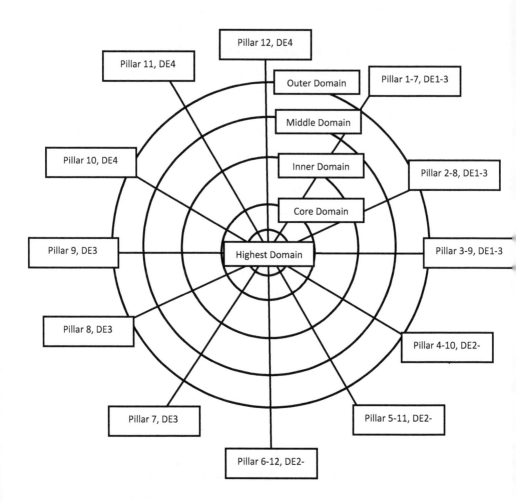

The pillars unfold within each domain, where different aspects of the template, energy system and organic vessel are developed. All within the respective reality fields, using the dimensional energies. Density 5 and dimensions 13-15 are not for all.

Making a Human
The 6 pillars and their outposts and worlds, unfolding from the high-technological core domain constructions, i.e. the Workstations, have their version of a genetic Library. These libraries hold the plasma vials with the genetic prototypes, which are the groundwork of the root races. A genetic consciousness unit is called a filament. Each filament is a blend of one consciousness unit and its proper holographic coding in an energetic casing.

A human template is first built holographically, using a replica of the genetic filaments of that root race along with the archetype of the organic vessel matching the progressive human prototype looked-for in that world. These are also stored in the local Library. After this, individual add-ons are inserted to make it personal. The additions are transferred from the previous template, energy system and organic vessel into the new, and then the outdated organic vessel and energy system etc. are dissolved.

The Pillar Set Up and Root Races
Pillar 1-7 (Root Race 1 - Evolutionary Cycle 1)
Develops the individual aspect of the consciousness units, using the energies of density 1, 2 and 3 to do so, through the progression spiral of dimension 1-7, in several stages of dimension 1-3 (DE1), D4-6 (DE2) and completing in dimension 7 (DE3).

Pillar 2-8 (Root Race 2 - Evolutionary Cycle 2)
Develops the racial or group aspect of the consciousness units, using the energies of density 1, 2 and 3 to do so, through the progression spiral of dimension 2-8, in several stages of dimension 2-3 (DE1), D4-6 (DE2), D7 (DE3) and completing in dimension 8 (DE3).

Pillar 3-9 (Root Race 3 - Evolutionary Cycle 3)
Develops the reality field aspect of the consciousness units, using the energies of density 1, 2 and 3 to do so, through the progression spiral of dimension 3-9, in several stages of dimension D3 (DE1), D4-6 (DE2), D7-8 (DE3) and completing in dimension 9 (DE3).

Pillar 4-10 (Root Race 4 - Evolutionary Cycle 4)
Develops the systemic aspect of the consciousness units, using the energies of density 2, 3 and 4 to do so, through the progression spiral of dimension 4-10, in several stages of dimension D4-6 (DE2), D7-9 (DE3) and completing in dimension 10 (DE4).

Pillar 5-11 (Root Race 5 - Evolutionary Cycle 5)
Develops the holographic-technological aspect of the consciousness units, using the energies of density 2, 3 and 4 to do so, through the progression spiral of dimension 5-11, in several stages of dimension 5-6 (DE2), D7-9 (DE3) D10 (DE4) and completing in dimension 11 (DE4).

Pillar 6-12 (Root Race 6 - Evolutionary Cycle 6)
Develops the universal aspect of the consciousness units, using the energies of density 2, 3 and 4 to do so, through the progression spiral of dimension 6-12, in several stages of dimension 6 (DE2), D7-9 (DE3) D10-11 (DE4) and completing in dimension 12 (DE4).

The NGC Expands the Old Setup
The original mechanics are reestablished into all progressive realities that still have selections of the original 12 human lineages as the NGC rolls over all universes. The transition work will unfold as the stages of the NGC get completed and new realities will ignite as the old worlds transform and progress into their highest standards. When the NGC

humans have developed their pillars, they merge into new groups as part of the 6-12 pillar to begin the NGC 6th root race. This 6th root race will develop the programs and standards for the new universal cycles, where all universal realms will be completed.

- The new core domains in density 6, dimensions 16-18, will hold the highest developed humans to set the standards of the next rounds and cycles. Will be developed in all universal systems through the 6-12 pillars and the future 6th to 7th root races.
- The new highest domain in density 7, dimensions 19-21, will hold the next potentials of the eternal unified consciousness fields.

The NGC 7 evolutionary cycles
- 7 cycles of existence developing life, consciousness and energy.
- 12 consciousness genetic lineages unfolded in root races 1-7.
- 7 domains of human existence within dimensions 1-21.
- Densities 1-7 following the domains and cycles of existence. *Density 1 will phase out as density 7 comes into existence and a new outer domain is established in density 2.*

To Sum Up
- The root races develop through a dynamic of going from the low-energy worlds to the high-energy worlds, using the dimensions of the progression spiral to do so, where one is begun and one is completed in each cycle.
- Each dimension is a plane of existence, or a world, with a specific organic vessel and energy system and via the coding of the template, corresponds to the 5 domains.
- Pillar 6-12 is the last round of the pillar work, when cycle 6, root race 6 have been completed in the joint NGC progression work (after completing the first 5 root races and 5 cycles to catch up with the

original energies and standards), then the succeeding root races will begin to transition into the final 7th cycle.

- In the 7th cycle, all the root races cluster up in one of the main pillars of their choice. Here they get ready for the final stages of the cycles in the pillars 7 to 12 (DE3-DE4) to get a position within the upcoming groups of human races, in the new cycles, with the progression rate they have accomplished.

- As the last 7th cycle is completed, the ones that have accomplished all levels of the 10th, 11th and 12th pillars, will seed the highest level of the continuing consciousness units in the new highest domain. These humans will set the highest purity rate, the highest standards and the highest progression rate for the next evolutionary cycles.

- The other pillars in the rings of progression will be reset, according to the new human standards, into new planes of existence where the templates and energy systems of the previous cycles can accomplish what was not achieved in the previous evolutionary cycles.

On the Original Humans and the Impure Genetics

The humans of the original highest domain were the ones that went to the Ancient Ones and got acknowledged to unfold the continuation of the 12 universal human lineages within the reality constructions of the Ancient Ones. By this act, they defined the highest progression rate for us that joined the project. These original humans entered from other universes and cycles with their consciousness genetics and organic vessels.

In many ways, this group of original humans do not deserve any veneration. The genetic filaments they used to produce the genetic prototype of the 12 lineages held spores of 3rd cycle impurities. It should have been detected in the selection of the genetic filaments (3 of the vials had spores of 3rd cycle genetics – only 9 were pure) and when it was, a purification should have been instigated, but it did not.

48

These impurities led to unforeseen genetic consciousness mutations, which hindered the correct actions to be taken as the experiments with the 3rd cycle energies took place in the Sirian Workstations. Due to the impure genetics, a craving for 3rd cycle energies led to more desires, and eventually infusions with 3rd cycle energy went into the resonance grids of the Sirius system and created the timeline event.

The timeline event led to a reversal of multiple timelines, making them run backwards while producing regression and inertia, instead of moving forwards and allowing for the progression work to unfold. The majority of the people on Sirius C got fragmented and scattered backwards into the 3rd cycle because of their overly use of mechanical technologies. Reality sections from Sirius A and B went into the future cycles of the Sirius system, carrying the impurities.[5]

Anyways, most of the original humans have moved on. To ensure the continuation of the human lineages, they have stored a version of their original organic forms, energy systems and templates in the core facilities, if further genetic filaments are needed for replication.[6]

It should be noted that 3 of the original organic vessels had the impurities of the 3rd cycle energies, since they were the contributors of the plasma vials with prototype filaments. These 3 originals, called Primes, have been evaporated to extinguish further impurities within the 12 human lineages and root races, they were the primes of, i.e. within plasma vials the pillars 2-8, 4-10 and 5-11.

---

[5] The mutation in the code sheets is called *the Leviathan genome*, and it generates the code sequences in the energy system that develop the black snakes in all humans holding reptoid-human genetics from the Sirius system. The Leviathan genome generates the dark residual energies, aka the black goo, from where the snakes grow. The black goo connects to the 3rd cycle grids in the dark-verses and alters the entire energy system into a dark light system taking energy instead of radiating it. The dark-verses are the long-gone and done reality fields of the left-behind 3rd cycle that went into darkness as it was completed and all consciousness moved on.

[6] Replication is normal for the higher order worlds. It preserves the original prototype and at the same time a replication has all the correct coding.

The ATE Reality Zones

After the timeline event, happening sometime during the early stages of the first Atlantis (Atlantis had 5 versions), the outer and the middle domains were divided into *new reality zones*, where the infected root races could do their restoring and transformation work back into the standards of the progressive worlds. Our system became the place of *the restoration programs* aka the ISP (the hijacked program behind present day base program) and the LPU second chance programs (the Cross[7] and the Pentagram[8]), which were developmental programs made to enable a transition back into the BTE settings of the original progressive 5 domains.

The 6-12 pillar in our system remained with the original energies of the progressive worlds for a long time. It was so, because the 6-12 pillar did not get affected by the timeline event, that happened in the 5-11 pillar, although the other pillars below did. However, none of the fine restoration plans saw a completion due to the all-over resistance from the regressed races. They had adjusted to the ATE realities and had these under their control and the 6-12 pillar were shut down to protect the highest levels of our reality. It had to be so to protect the core facilities and the genetic Library of the 12 universal lineages, in their upmost purified version.

From this look into the past, let us move into the present.

---

[7] The developmental program called the Cross was created by the Sirian B and As, the Pleadians and the avian-human Arcturians, and set in motion in Atlantis 1 to restore humans with the Leviathan genome. At the same time the contamination, i.e. from the fragmentation of the ancient worlds that were blown up in the timeline event, were growing because of experiments done by the Niburians – under the Pentagram - creating the 2D Underworld. The combination of the fragmented genetics and the infection became impossible to stop. The infected dark creatures, of the long-gone worlds of the 3rd cycle, are in 1D.

[8] The Cross and the Pentagram developmental programs are explained in detail in *Modern History*.

The Unfolding of the NGC into Our System

What is a cycle and how does it work in our system? Let us investigate that before moving into the understanding of the new grand cycle.

Science anticipate that all energetic changes in our reality run in a linear fashion, probably because they view our planet as a closed environmental system with few or limited feed-back dynamics, and they have in-calculated that in their prognosis of the changes to come and how much time humans have got to do the transition.

However, the energetic changes do not run in a linear fashion, given that they are the manifestation of extra-systemic energies from other-dimensional realities. All of which are levels of reality, science do not understand yet, let alone that these hidden dimensions affect our world in higher order scientific ways. Consequently, every single calculation done by sciences, building upon the notion of only a few dimensions of reality, are more or less incorrect.

All energetic changes, such as erratic weather patterns, the ebbs and flows of the water tides, the energies in volcanic activity, the movement of the tectonic plates, the subduction mechanics, the possibility and probability rates in the quantum fields, the magnetic polar shifts, the solar cycles, the virtual discharges in atomic fields and appearances of new clusters, the cyclic changes in nature, the development and mutations in lifeforms, the opening and closing of dormant DNA, the bacterial and microbial activation and similar micro and macro energetic systems, are all governed by *the extra-systemic cycles of change*. The extra-systemic cycles of change originate from realities beyond present-day understanding. Realities composed of other-dimensional worlds and density systems inhabited by advanced progressive human and the less progressive humanoid races, living in highly advanced systems beyond the accepted level of science. Our universe might look depleted and devoid of any forms of life, but only in the atomic section of it, i.e. the accepted 3rd dimension with the dynamics of space-time, relativity and the speed of light as the ruling vectors of change.

The extra-systemic cycles of change run exponentially and cycle in and out of our field and matter reality,[9] amplifying each other when they enter. And this time around, they carry with them the energies of the NGC. *The extra-systemic energies*, driving the cycles, build up and reinforce similar energies in other sections of the fields, be it on a quantum, atomic or molecular level. In the beginning, the extra-systemic energy appears with unnoticeable changes in selected nodal points within the minor grids, in a series of smaller cyclic changes, and later on with major cyclic energies into the main grids.

The extra-systemic energies can be alleviated and implemented to generate productive changes, and allow for higher order levels of reality unfold. This is the natural way in all progressive systems.

Progressive systems are built upon changes, and the willingness to instigate changes. Contrary to our current world setup that is built upon status quo systems to keep our solar system stuck in the density 1 (D1-3). Therefore, if the smaller cycles of change are not met in the correct manner and implemented into the energetic fields governing our reality and additionally integrated into the human energy system, utilizing the extra-systemic cyclic energies for individual and collective

---

[9] Our reality is composed of fields of energy, which are holographic in nature. The holographic resonance fields hold the possibilities to unfold as energetic waves or particles, i.e. the higher order code systems to generate light and matter. Change the code systems and the properties of waves and particles will change from their density 1 version (D1-3) into a density 2 (D4-6) version, where waves and particles can take on 4th dimensional features. Once that happens, the human consciousness-energy interaction potentials will be restored.

progression,[10] the incoming energies of the major cycles will build up to disruptive heights and instead of instigating long-needed changes, they generate disaster. Which they already are. And, there are several cycles of change to be completed in our solar system in this present age, given that the old systemic cycles are coming to an end.

Subsequently, our reality and everything in it do not change in a step by step manner, where humans can do what they need to do in the slow pace, they prefer. It changes accordingly to the larger extra-systemic changes beyond our human control. The only thing humans can control, is to follow the great leaps of change or to resist them.

Nonetheless, as we know, selected groups of humanity have been in for a rough awakening for some time now, although any attempted implementation of the extra-systemic energies are moving too slow to meet up with the systemic changes. Mainly because most of these good-intended groups were used by the extra-systemic races in our system, which are not really in for the changes, but knew they had to face up to some of them to keep status quo and to be able to control the incoming energies.[11] We are seeing the small effects of the none to incorrect implementation now – and more disruptive occurrences will arise as the NGC extra-systemic energies escalate exponentially, especially as long as there are no humans to implement the energies correctly. This is how it works.

---

[10] All of my work is an attempt to teach these sciences.

[11] The anti-progression races could control the extra-systemic energies when these entered into the minor grids. A delay that was done by relooping the reality grids into a previous probability rate of energy (a previous branch of the timeline). But when the energies will hit the major grids in the years of 2020-2025, it will not be possible to halt the dynamics or delay any further. As the major grids begin to activate and reset, all of the nodal points in the timelines belonging to the old cycles will dissipate, including all branches of alternate realities. A fact that has led to a huge withdrawal of the other extra-systemic races, taking off while they could. However, since our universe is part of a very big universal community of races, there are still many of the lesser progressive races left in our system doing business as usual as long as they can.

The Stages of the NGC

The new grand cycle (the NGC) unfolds over several decades to fully complete its sequences of activation and closing down of the many reality fields, which are deemed failed or are too distorted to repair. The NGC began in the progressive systems some 2550 years ago, and it has worked its way down to us ever since.

In 1959 the initial energies of the NGC hit our sun and began the shift into a 4-6th dimensional sun. In 2007 the sun began the process of shedding off the DE1 (D1-3) layers.

In 2022 the sun will initiate the transformation of its DE2 level to meet up with the energetic settings of the NGC, which will affect our solar system and us energetically.[12] The NGC began *the activation and cleanup stages of the completion cycles* in 1999 and they are entirely completed in 2135. In 2235 the DE1 (D1-3) levels will be no more.

The Activation and Cleanup Stages of the Completion Cycles

1999-2007: Activation and cleanup of the holographic-technological segments of the minor and major grids within the 5-11 pillar.

2008-2016: Activation and cleanup of the systemic segments of the minor and major grids within the 4-10 pillar.

2017-2025: Activation and cleanup of the reality field segments of the minor and major grids within the 3-9 pillar.

2026-2034: Activation and cleanup of the racial and library segments of the minor and major grids within the 2-8 pillar.

2035-2043: Activation and cleanup of the individual segments of the minor and major grids within the 1-7 pillar.

---

[12] The need for all humans to become herbivore is crucial in this. As the sun changes its energetic settings, only humans having an organic bio-field, living on a plant-based diet, will be able to process the energies of the sun. The organic bio-field on a plant-based diet will adapt and become able to process the energies of the sun in a similar fashion as plants, i.e. the process of photosynthesis to assimilate the energies of the sun.

The Final Stages of the Completion Cycles
2044-2052: Completion and Choices to be Made (stay or go)
2053-2061: The Reseeding of the 6th Root Race will Begin
2062-2135: The Final Grid Shift into the Progressive Worlds
2135-2235: The Evaporation of the DE1 Solar System

The completion cycles run over periods of 9 years, where each period begins the activation and cleanup of the energies and genetics in the holographic grids and resonance fields connected to each of the pillars of the Workstations. Then the energies enter the core of the planets in our system, and outwards into the realms of the DE1 universe.

The last to be activated are the DE1 organic lifeforms in the individual 1-7 pillar cycle in 2035-2043 and this process is followed by a period of 9 years in 2044-2052, where humanity – now with a very large group aware of higher order worlds - can choose to stay and do the required transition into a DE2 progressive human or choose to move into the segregated worlds under the regressed races. This choice will be done by the higher dimensional version connected to the human within our reality. As the years go by more humans will activate and remember what they truly are. This is not the "higher self" that activates, but the true self, so to speak.

However, many humans remain within the DE1 segment and continue to exist in the depleting and slowly dying solar system. More on the future human solar system nations in a later chapter.

Naturally, a lot of relooping from the regressed has been attempted to prevent the different levels to complete their activation and clean-up processes in our system. However, the stages will be completed, slowly but surely by the continuous counter relooping by the councils.

Now, what an activation and cleanup process actually is needs to be clarified, because there seem to be uncertainty about what it entails. I will use an allegory to explain this.

The activation process is to be likened with an old house. Nobody can remember when it was built and by who. An unattended garden and a lot of wasted wilderness surround the house, because the land and the garden have not been attended to in a long time and everything has gone unorganized. The house has been left to its own demise as well, since the true owners left ages ago and the foundation and the building materials of the house have grown into a small world full of bugs, termites and all sorts of creepy stuff, ranging from old energies and furniture of the ones that used to live there, to foreign tenants, having occupied the house without any good intentions at heart. For all that they have cared, the house and its land are just another place to exploit and tear down in the process of getting what they need.

Now, when the process of activation hits non-attended levels of reality – which our system is highly affected by, i.e. we have not attended any of the levels of our reality for at least 12500 years but have left it to the hijackers to do what they felt like doing here – it means a big clean up, and all that needs to be removed, to reset the reality fields, must go.

The foreign tenants must go as the first most important step, because they are trashing the house and their energy is allowing for all sorts of bugs to be present in the house, the garden and the land. After the tenants are gone, the big work of getting the house, the garden and the land back on its feet begins. However, the correct rebuilding is only possible if the true owners come back, take responsibility for this work and do their part.

But, regrettably, the true owners have forgotten how to take care of a house, a garden and how to develop the surrounding land. They are like children having lived in a bubble of deception and false notions of reality, and what is important.

Because of that, they have forgotten their true skills of masonry, of gardening and of how to make land prosper. These skills have to be remembered and relearned through trial and error. The true owners have to learn it all over again how to repair their house and what the architecture is behind it, so that the rebuilding is done according to the original blueprint and the purpose of the house. They have to learn how to do gardening and about the plants and their purpose, and they have to relearn how to grow the soil of the land, and how to make it prosper for future generations. All of their folly ideas of what is important must be transformed into a mature perception of what is true, just and eternal.

The Last Grand Transition of the Solar System

In the year 2135 the regressed races will have been segregated from the progressive worlds. The progressive worlds will continue with the 6th dimension as the basic plane of organic-energetic existence. After this point, none of the segregated worlds can reenter, since they are all positioned within the 4th to 5th dimensions (regressed DE2). None of the regressed races want to maintain what is within dimension 1-3 (DE1), so that will fade away in their systems too.

This means that in the year 2135 all the rings of progression in our system can be reset to default, and that is the plan.

The changes following the NGC allow for the original progression work of the 12 human lineages into the 6-12 pillar, which means that the current 1-7 to 5-11 pillars will undergo transformation as well, uplifting these to new potentials and eventually reset them to a new standard as part of the new evolutionary cycles.

The DE1 (D1-3) realities will be the last to experience the changes and only the ones that are at the same radiation and vibration levels of the NGC will be able to detect these changes in the years to come. For the rest, our solar system will look as desolated as it has up until now – especially if it is perceived through the DE1 perspective.

In 2135 the resonance fields in our solar system will be changed from the inside and out to adjust to the new settings of all universes. This means that all races in our solar system will be transformed into a changed human prototype with the 6th dimension as the template and energy standard to be met as the first step. The Workstations will be prepared for the new categories of consciousness, enabling the new human root races to step into new energetic reality fields within the rearranged domains, dimensions and density fields. After this, the progression plan of the 12 human lineages, to unfold and complete within 21 dimensions, can be accomplished following the standards of the 7 evolutionary cycles of this era.

So, to get humanity to where they should be – according to the design of the NGC and the completion cycles – the below have been decided by the higher order councils in late 2019.

- Full intervention protocol from 2020-2021. Perhaps longer.
- Emplacement into 5 reality zones for the remaining section of the 3-9 pillar completion cycle.

Similar efforts to emplace humanity in the first two completion cycles have been tried, but every time the attempts have been intersected by the regressed races. Consequently, this time the regressed races have been put under intervention protocol. This will give humanity the best chances to do their activation and cleanup work, and benefit from it. So, what does an intervention and emplacement actually entail?

The Emplacement in 2020-2021

While the NGC is doing its work with the grids and resonance fields, upgrading and changing these in the last section of years in the 3-9 pillar completion cycle from 2020-2025, the councils have instigated *intervention protocol* to ensure a correct completion of the activation sequences and pillar cleanup. This is contrary to what happened in the activation cycles of the 5-11 pillar and the 4-10 pillar, where the higher order councils trusted the regressed to follow the design of the completion cycles. Instead, as we know, the visiting regressed extra-systemic humanoids and the remaining intra-systemic races relooped and halted the completion cycles to the infinite, in order to prevent the incoming energies of the NGC to get grounded into the grids.

And, at the same time, the regressed races prevented all humans, living within their jurisdictions, in doing the activation work that could have gotten humanity much further in their awakening process and by that would have been able to contain the energies of the NGC.

Therefore, the years 2020-2021 unfold under the intervention protocol to allow for the NGC energies to do their work, which means:

- Seclusion of jurisdictions belonging to the regressed races and by that keeping them within their own grids. This stops them from entering the reality zones and areas, which can absorb the NGC energies and in that assist our reality in upgrading.

- All human-humanoid programs will be shut down and humans with hybrid templates, will be cleared of the engineered genetic combinations.

- These humans are reinstated genetically into what the template indicates of original content, before the overlay genetic hybrid insertions. The rest is for the human to clear out.

- An isolation of the human mental field, the emotional field and bio-organic field to avoid any further interruption of a possible awakening processes. By isolating all humans within their lower fields, they will not be exposed to parasitic or energetic transfer from other humans. Every man and every woman can then work with what is truly his or hers.

- Along with massive infusions of energy to activate the resonance grids in the different segments.

Following the years in 2020-2021, humanity will be emplaced into *5 reality zones*. The calculation for this will be according to what they were, what they have become and what they have the possibility to activate. We will then have humans within the 5 groups:

1. Humans with regressed templates and genetics, and therefore in essence are humans with regressed souls aka a regressed.
2. Humans and templates that will phase out under the extinction protocol, because they hold no viable genetics.
3. Humans that will try and make it in the DE1 i.e. all humans not aware of the higher order worlds, or the regressed worlds.
4. Humans working to enter the rehabilitation zone and afterwards doing the work to enter the progressive worlds within the pillar, they belong to, when their rehabilitation work is done.
5. Humans that knowingly continue the progression work, they got derailed from during either Atlantis or Lemuria and by their own accord can work their way back into the 6-12 pillar.

After 2021 all templates and energy systems (and thus humans) will be emplaced into the 5 reality zones according to what they appear to be energetically, genetically and according to the pillar level, they reached a long time ago. This will determine what is to be relearned to meet the NGC requirements. The sum of genetics that can activate and their forms of energies are calculated to emplace the template and its code sequences into the correct segments.

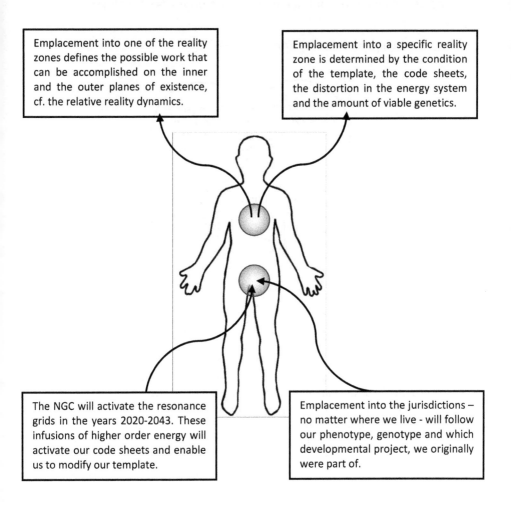

Emplacement into one of the reality zones defines the possible work that can be accomplished on the inner and the outer planes of existence, cf. the relative reality dynamics.

Emplacement into a specific reality zone is determined by the condition of the template, the code sheets, the distortion in the energy system and the amount of viable genetics.

The NGC will activate the resonance grids in the years 2020-2043. These infusions of higher order energy will activate our code sheets and enable us to modify our template.

Emplacement into the jurisdictions – no matter where we live - will follow our phenotype, genotype and which developmental project, we originally were part of.

The 5 Human Reality Zones

To ensure the most optimal result of the NGC, our reality, templates and energy systems have been divided into 5 reality zones to provide the best chances of continuing within the progressive realities.

Our Earth and its 5 Reality Zones 2020-2043:

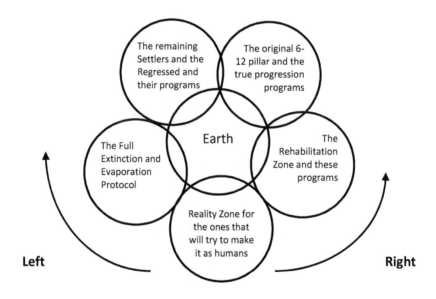

Humans will be emplaced into the reality zone, they belong to. This can be figured out by observing what is happening in and around them, as well as to what degree the incentive is to do the awakening process, the level of self-reached information and the ability to do advanced energy work. The more viable genetics there are in the template, the more natural a self-instated awakening process is. The left and right follow the chiasm. After 2021 we can change our emplacement by doing the work, but it will become increasingly more difficult as the NGC completes it sequences.

The Chiasm Now and Onward

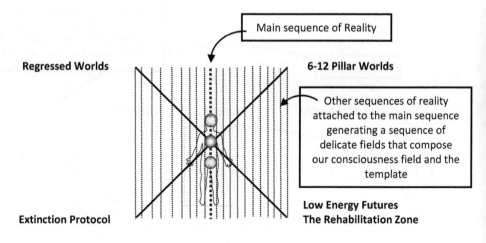

Please notice that the sequences are not correctly illustrated since the slices of reality we are composed of, are in the numbers of infinity.

In other words, we can through the chiasm and its perception field:

1) Undo all regressed imprints, fields and consciousness genetics stuck in the older cycles and timelines we have participated in, willingly or unwillingly.

2) Undo the genetic regression and restore the template.

3) Undo the distortion of the genetics and restore them.

4) Develop the correct genetic composition of our bio-field and in this enable us to build more genetics into our physical form.

5) Regain conscious access to the other reality zones.

6) Undo the regression in our template and the code sequences, separating us from the progressive human worlds, and regain full conscious accessibility.

7) Remove all prohibiting technologies, their fields, genetics and energetic to semi-organic parasites.

The Progressive Energy System

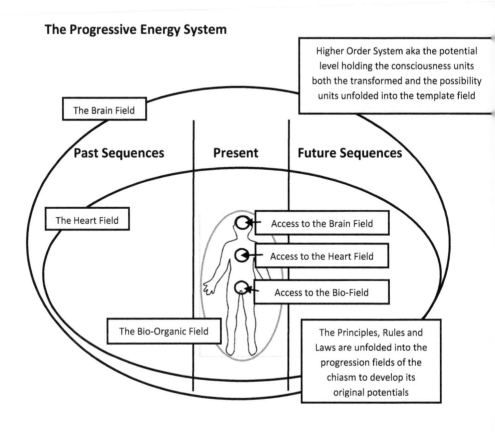

The human energy system is built up of different fields composed of codes sequences, energy units and consciousness units.

The progressive energy system can be worked with through the access points entering the heart field, the brain field and the bio-organic field after having cleared out and removed the lower order fields. Then the reconstruction work with the vibration and radiation fields can begin. We use the code sequences stored in the template to do that.

The conscious and daily awareness process utilizing and following the Principles, the Rules and the Laws will alter the energetic state of the entire energy system, allowing it to reconnect to the template.

The Solar System Nations

The last piece of the reality puzzle are the human solar system nations and their operations within our world past, present and future. They are technically "the ones that will try and make it in the DE1." What are they and how did they arise as a future group of DE1 humans?

In the future after the completion cycles are over, the humans that do not end up transferring into the progressive DE2 worlds or choose to join the extra-systemic hybrid humanoid-human races on the visible 5th dimensional quantum based crystalline new earth, engineered for the purpose within the Andromeda galaxy, will continue their human existence in our solar system as part of what is called the solar system nations.

The solar system nations (the SSN) originate from an initial group of humans, taking part of the solar system nations program 1, which began their space exploration programs around the year 2149-2154 on this timeline. This selected group of humans hibernated for a long time in 3 space stations as our solar system underwent the resetting and convulsion cycles, within the evaporation phases of the NGC.

The changes of our solar system will in the future become evident as the severe effects of the NGC change the conditions on our planet into non-habitable. The fusion processes of the old version of our sun will turn erratic and the solar storms grow increasingly stronger, topped with a declining magnetic field around our planet. It will become clear that the sun is undergoing a process that cannot support a continued human civilization in our system, and at that point in time, humanity get their sciences in order to find the solutions for a continuation of the human race further out in our solar system and beyond.[13]

The solar system nations we know of on our timeline, as they return from the future, are therefore positioned in a dying solar system in the probability fields of the year 2750 and onward in a cold, dark and desolated empty space,[14] within a section of the 3D-4D, harnessing deep space energy to survive and sustain their space stations.

The First SSN Program

The group of humans, of the first program, were chosen due to their DNA composition and all from the intra-systemic human programs.

They were trained to live in space and taught the true sciences to be able to survive in the altered conditions, all of which were done in future covert programs similar to what we have seen so far.

The first SSN program involved a bio-altering process consisting of a complicated DNA modification program that allowed for extended periods of time in space. However, the SSN modification technologies are not from the future, but were invented ages ago in the next-door

---

[13] It must not be forgotten that the intra-systemic human lineages up until that point were vouching for their technologies in this, being sure they would find the solutions to continue their existence within the DE1 solar system and outside the progressive worlds, including keeping up the veil of deception to prolong their own existence. But at that time, it is clear that they cannot continue their existence within this system by the use of their outdated DE1 and DE2 technologies. Hence the implementation of their technologies into our world as the last attempt to continue their programs here.

[14] As the sun sheds off the DE1 layers, it will move into the 4th dimension and the old shell of what used to be our sun will remain within the DE1 until it turns into a white dwarf and then finally into a black dwarf. This process is what has happened to most of the stars and planets in our universe, when the holographic grids and core facilities stop supporting the DE1. And then all turns into a cold deep space, similar to that of the 3rd cycle, where everything is left to decay and evaporate. In essence, our solar system – as the higher order worlds move on with the NGC – is pushed fully into the 3rd cycle after the NGC. We are half there already.

realities belonging to the intra-systemic lineages, but they will appear within our present-day world in the near future. The effectuation of these sciences into our world allow for an application of DE2 hybrid gene-altering technologies into the human sciences, which then will support the human-humanoid crystalline programs within our reality. The SSN modification technologies will give the impression of being a continuation of existing gene drive technology.[15]

The SSN Modification Technologies
In the near future, new groups of quadruple elements are discovered and from that, new forms of enzymes can be engineered to affect the human biology. With this apparently new gene technology the human cells can be modified in new ways. It is done via *a hyperbolic enzymic elevation* within a selection of gene sequences, enabling these to be coupled to a higher-dimensional humanoid gene spiral. The way into the human helix is through the dormant action potentials, which can be upgraded and modified into fitting together with various forms of extra-systemic genetics.

In the modification process[16] the hyperbolic enzymes are injected, via holographic field transfer,[17] and the messenger RNA (m-RNA) can

---

[15] Read about GDT https://en.wikipedia.org/wiki/Gene_drive

[16] Done in a space with no gravity (alteration chambers), on board crafts or in intra-systemic or extra-systemic facilities positioned in the 4th dimension.

[17] The organic vessel is elevated into a 4th dimensional state. In that state the energy system of a human can be temporarily released from the organic vessel and worked on holographically. This is possible because of the 4th dimensional properties and dynamics. All races use this technology to alter the gene sequences of an organic vessel and to upgrade the template. The difference is, in progressive systems, that we do it ourselves using the technology, we have engineered for the purpose, and therefore we are in control of the modification. In our system, it is done without any forms of consent, and it is not for the benefit of the true owner of the organic vessel. The use here is illegal, which is why it is mostly executed by the means of androids to avoid the genetic ramifications of breaking the laws of our system, cf. the regression spiral dynamics.

be rewritten and made into replicating the DNA information in a new way. Instead of replicating the current downsized state of the human DNA, which replicate within a selection of possible code sequences to keep it within the 3rd dimensional setting, the chosen sequence of the human gene code replicates itself into a state similar to the humanoid sequences that can process 4th dimensional energy.

The double strand-double helix technology adds a second spiral to the original helix. The duplex pair of helices subsequently consist of a helix with human DNA within this reality spliced together with a humanoid spiral with humanoid genetics within the 4th or higher dimension.

This technology has been used extensively within the human projects for ages. E.g. the double helix technology is what has allowed for the attachment of the "higher self." The higher self is an older version of extra-systemic misuse of an organic vessel within our reality, done by a race that has no rights to be here and thus cannot take on a human or animal vessel in the correct ways.

By the modification of the organic DNA, by adding it with a duplex spiral done in the 4th dimension or onboard crafts, an extra-systemic humanoid can attach its other-dimensional genetics and template to the human or animal organic vessel and from that be able to operate within our reality.

In cases, where the human discovers the extra-systemic operator, the humanoid – very often an insectoid, avian or reptoid - has presented itself as being a benefactor or the higher self to convince the human to consent to the unlawful use of his or her organic form.

68

Taking on an organic vessel is complicated and demands allowances in the Library as well as an implementation into the racial grids, so the double helix technology became the solution for the humanoid races to be able to do their illegal genetic trade businesses in our system.

The side effects of the duplex technology are the energetic parasites, which are produced in the lower fields as the subsequent residuals of the wrongful use of an organic form, and ultimately the humanoid has to detach because of elevated states of distortion.

The same technology was used in ancient times to attach the nagas,[18] which are a type of advanced parasitic Sirian A TEGs[19] employed in the ancient worlds to bestow the kings and rajas, priests and gurus the abilities to communicate directly with and receive guiding information from their extra-systemic overlord. Naturally, in these days, presented to be the revered god or gods.

The 4th dimensional energy is today known as dark energy and dark matter but as the quadruple chemical elements are discovered, the 4th dimension is acknowledged as a reality field with dissimilar dynamics that affect matter and energy in new ways.

The mathematics and the 4D holographic vector sciences will then be developed and by the use of the 4D holographic vector technologies, the modification technologies can be implemented into our world as something humans have invented. These sciences are then followed up by quantum technologies of how to harness deep space energy and modify it into fuel, allowing for extreme long periods of time in space.

---

[18] In ancient Egypt as cobras and in India etc. as nagas.
[19] The TEGs – technologically enhanced genetics - are explained in both *the Souls of Humanity* and *Terralogy*.

The Human Made Androids

The future space stations are operated by human made androids. The android prototype will be developed in Japan, using titanium for the skeleton and geranium to create the semi-organic coating, along with the interior liquid light technologies (the LLT).

The liquid light technologies are *DNA infused wave energy or light* within silicate cords built up of *liquid chip nanotechnology,* creating an artificial bio-metric silicate brain and central nervous system (CNS).

The DNA sequences, used in the LLT, are similar to the sequences found in the egg and sperm of the human species, although added with replicated and edited insectoid or avian genetics. The insectoid genetics are chosen for their properties of a controllable hive-mind response to energetic impulses from outer electromagnetic sources to precure a controllable functionality of the bio-metric silicate brain.

The artificial CNS in the androids are mainly built from replicated avian genetics. The avian genetics are chosen to simulate an internal navigation system that can detect spatial features and the field lines of the magnetic field to generate the upside-down ability all lifeforms have, i.e. to be positioned correctly to where they are on the planet and understand where they are on the planet as well. The androids are, in the future, maneuvered by *quantum information processing systems* and *augmented adaptation technology (the AAT).*

*Artificial intelligence, as we have seen it so far, will be abandoned in the future due to too high risk of dysfunctionality, similar to a virus in computer programs and the ability to hack these. The artificial entities of the future are not AI (unless AI is **A**lien **I**nvasion technology, then it is correct). The augmented adaptation technologies will take over, using the artificially produced DNA in all simulation and interactive modalities to run machines etc. The liquid chip nanotechnologies play a pivotal role in this to create the needed interior network for the AAT.*

However, the replicated DNA of the androids will be solely within *the neutron spectrum* and is a fully edited version of the organic DNA, written in code systems with prohibitors, so that the neutrons cannot reconnect to the protons and electrons. It is called a locked-in system, where the replicated and edited DNA is prohibited to recreate its full composition by interfacing with the environment and there regain its original settings.[20]

The neutrons were chosen as the energetic driver of the androids due to the fact that the neutrons, because of their neutral charge, can be infused with the deep spaced harnessed energy.

The harnessed deep space energy (the DSE) is gathered into huge spheres, fueling the engines and technologies of the space stations, including the bio-metric system of the androids, i.e. their LLT. The DSE spheres also fuel the stasis chambers in the space stations as well as the reversed engineered android crafts, used in all encounters here.

Deep space energy (DSE) is a form of quantum energy that is part of the fabric of the DE1 universe. DSE is an energetic residual from big bang, i.e. the timeline event. The timeline event unfolded in density 2 and then ran backwards in time and created a huge fusion event at the horizon of our universe, as the density 2 energies hit the repulsion barrier of the original 3rd cycle. The fusion energy then looped back, infused with 3rd cycle energies (electromagnetic energy) and created what science see as big bang and the origin of our universe. In essence big bang is the beginning of our universe, because the timeline event transformed the energetic properties of our universe into a 3rd cycle composition, slightly merged with density 2 (D4-6) energies, creating the current version of the DE1 in which we live.

---

[20] Without going further into this, the environmental interface mechanics (such as epigenetic changes in biological systems) will be discovered, when the dynamics of quantum tunneling and entanglement in biological systems are fully understood.

Coming Back from the Future

The surviving group of humans from the SSN program 1 travelled back in time and reconnected their *future human identity signature* to the organic vessel they had in this timeline, around the 1950's or so, and they have enhanced their children with liquid light technology and inserted hyperbolic DNA. These children are the participants of the SSN program 2 within our timeline. The majority of these children are found within innovative companies and similar private contractors, dealing with inventive future technology and sciences. All to push the future technologies into an earlier date.

Another group of children in our timeline, within a sub-section of the SSN program 2, are called *the Golden Orb Children*. These children were artificially inseminated into a carefully chosen group of females, without their consent and primarily descending from the regressed races within the human population, to bring about the next stage of the enhanced DNA. The main goal of the inseminations was to seed the enhanced DNA into the collective bio-field of humanity and with that allowing for new upgrades in the SSN modification technologies following the SSN program 2 group that will return from their future timelines and enter into their past human version within our timeline.

The goal of the SSN program 2 is to upgrade the ancestral DNA of their lineages. Naturally, within clandestine programs and again using humans unknowingly for their genetic experiments to attain the DNA sequences, they need. The purpose is to reach the other dimensions outside the evaporation zones, housing their present location in deep space, and reconnect to the future realities of the regressed races, which they encountered in the first program in deep space.

Thus, the future humans and their androids have been part of the enhanced human projects, going on here since the 1970's in secret space programs under the NOA assemblies, creating the technologies of the future to upgrade the first program, where only a small portion survived. In essence, their programs are centered around eugenics or racial DNA purification and how to attain the perfect DNA sequence for any adaptation.

The process of making the next prototype of space stations and hibernation pods have been developed in underwater facilities, since the late 2000's. The deep oceanic space stations are positioned here, because the abyss provides the best conditions to simulate space and enables their technologies to cross the 3D space-time barrier into the 4th and 5th dimension.[21]

The Cycle of Devastation
The first SSN humans have already done *the cycle of devastation*, and they came back to ensure a larger portion would make it. First, they returned to perfect the SSN program 1 by upgrading themselves in an earlier time period, but failed. Instead they created the SSN program 2, making their children the next SSN generation, which eventually will return from the future and make further upgrades to their own children. They will fail as well, since DNA modification is only possible over several human generations.[22] A devastation cycle of attempts and failures that will run until the SSN program is a complete success.

However, as long as the SSN does not recognize the progressive worlds as an option, they are destined to fail – no matter how many times the SSN humans reattach to their former selves, while leaving behind their future organic vessel in stasis on the space stations. It is so, because they exist in the DE1 section of our universe, which goes under full extinction protocol in the near future. Naturally, a portion of the SSN humans will make it into the regressed worlds in the 4th

---

[21] I explain about NOA in *the Souls of Humanity* and their operations here.
[22] Short term genetic changes can be applied by the duplex technologies, but they are not lasting. Long term changes of the DNA take generations of humans, developing the new gene structure and applying its functionality into the biological molecules.

and 5th dimensions, but since the SSN humans are the descendants from the intra-systemic human lineages of our system,[23] this group will not make it in the regressed worlds. Only humanoids can live in their worlds. Enhanced humans or being a hybrid does not go well in the regressed worlds either, which the majority of the humanoid - human projects have experienced after several attempts to gain a local environment there. Hence the solution of their own world in the Andromeda system.

The circle of devastation for the SSN groups will repeat itself until they have learned the dynamics of the template, energy system and the higher worlds, they are part of and let go of their enhancement technologies. They have to choose to progress into the progressive worlds, their lineage originally came from eons ago, instead of their futile attempts to make it in the DE1.

If the SSN humans continue their trajectory of the 2750 timeline – although each program generates its own version of the first timeline - and the ideologies behind the SSN program, maintaining their deep space existence, they will eventually run out of energy and then turn into dust.

Now, from the present, let us focus on the progressive worlds again, and what we – as the original version of ourselves – had the possibility of having learned before the timeline event and the taking over of our reality.

---

[23] The SSN humans from the future have forgotten their ancestry, because as the first SSN program were initiated the intra-systemic human lineages were dying out. The intra-systemic races have that problem already, since their organic vessels – all from the ancient human projects under the Sirian As - are deteriorating. This is happening despite of their lives in the next-door realities, which are very similar to our world, albeit with very advanced cities, technologies etc.

Template Work & The First Two Pillars

How it Used to Be
In the old progression worlds there were no teachers of progression, since every human could - at all times - connect to the holographic teaching systems (the HTS) and there get the results of any choice to be made according to the Principles, the Rules and the Laws of that system, i.e. how the reality energies would work on the template in that type of density and reality, if we made that choice.

The holographic teaching systems were interactive and simulated possible scenarios according to the template, we had constructed and what we had decided to achieve in the system, we were part of.

If the possible futures were not of our liking (the HTS interacted with the chiasm, showing possible outcomes), we would change our ways or choose to recode our code sequences to fit the system, we were part of in a better way. We utilized our consciousness to do so, since we were the ones that had engineered our template and energy system, when we entered that system. Thus, if our template did not work, it was our responsibility to fix it.

Consequently, we are the only ones knowing how our template works and how it is engineered in detail. This is important to understand, because the underlying coding in everything we are, is something we have engineered. We learned that in the first two pillars.

We are sovereign in all that we are and we do not need teachers to make us become again. But we need other lifeforms and surroundings to mirror to us what we are, so we can self-correct and self-adjust.

Template Work & Racial DNA

- Some of the skills we learned in the 1-7 pillar, were all forms of template reconstruction, how to modify and upgrade the code sheets and how to program and repair our template. Along with the capacities of how to work with our energy system.

- In pillar 2-8 we learned how to develop the racial DNA, being a natural part of our template, so our alterations would be for the highest good of the many, i.e. for our race, or the race, we had chosen to be part of. In our individual progression work, we knew we affected the racial DNA too and we always developed our genetics in unity with the dynamics of interconnectedness, following *the Law of **the** One*, which means that if one can do it others can too, because everything we do gets implemented into the racial DNA.[24]

- In pillar 2-8, we also learned how to apply our knowledge and skills to accommodate for the highest progression rate of the system, we were part of. Meaning, that the main goal of our individual and collective progression work was to achieve what was for the highest good of the system, we were part of and at the same time accomplish what were looked-for to achieve our personal highest purity rate, highest standards and progression rate.

In the foundational pillar work, we learned all the hoped-for skills to exist correctly in the world, we had chosen to be part of. Some of the progression work, we could do on our own and other levels had to be

---

[24] That goes with the personal responsibility of always choosing what serves the highest good of the many, in our personal choices. What we do have an effect on the entire race. A progressive human is not local. He or she is global.

done as part of a group. We could attain the highest purity rate on our own, which was an organic-energetic exercise in the world, we were part of and how to exist in it correctly.

However, to achieve the highest standards required surroundings to interact with, such as other lifeforms and how to interact with them appropriately according to the system, we were in.[25] Only then would the vibration field, matching that system, get developed. And naturally, always by conferring to the Rules of Engagement used as a guideline of how to develop the vibration field to reach the most optimal solution, progression or development for all involved.

The highest progression rate, i.e. the work on the radiation field, involved projects based upon progression dynamics and the higher order sciences. Only by developing our surroundings in e.g. creational projects or community work would it be possible to reach the highest progression rate, since the projects we fashioned would show our abilities to work with the first 3 pillars as a progressive individual, as being part of a race and as a citizen in a progressive reality.

The above section has been written in past sentences. But, if we want to enter the rehabilitation zone, these skills are to be reactivated and integrated into our current life. We are to live this life, as if we were part of a progressive world.

Thus, the above and the below – as well as the next chapter – is not something "out there" or in the past, but something "in there" and in the now. It is knowledge that should be an integral part of who we are today, how we behave and how we manage ourselves and our life.

---

[25] All systems have their version of the Principles, Rules and Laws. Thus, the highest purity rate, the highest standards and the highest progression rate differ from system to system. It all depends on the holographic resonance fields and the kind of energy that is the prevailing in that system.

The General Templates

In the old days, before the systems fell into regression, it was possible to choose one of the general templates when entering into a system. We took what was us, energetically and genetically, and merged it with the general template of that system. That allowed us to create the accurate organic-energetic vessel of the new system, along with getting the pre-coded information of what would be expected of us in that system.[26]

But eventually, the individual preferences were added to achieve the highest progression rate etc., following our inclinations positioned in the highest levels of our being (the Word, the Vow and the Will) and what we had chosen to develop ourselves into.

The progressive races circulated within the progressive worlds to achieve the highest purity rate, the highest standards and the highest progression rate any system could offer. And we have had numerous functions, for the reason that we had specialized ourselves in various skills and abilities over the ages of our existence.

Ultimately, we would end up with one main specialty, we refined to perfection and we found systems and worlds that allowed for that specific skill and knowledge. When that was completed, we moved on into a new cycle, where we began afresh. But, before ending the old

---

[26] Many progressive races chose this in the old systems, when entering into another reality field, given that the general template was pre-coded with the information of what was required to perform appropriately in that reality. But, alas, that was one of the ways the progressive humans got manipulated when they entered a system that appeared progressive, but in fact had been infected and turned regressive. By taking on the general template, altered into a mixed template, they got under the regressed rules of polarization. Which of course, they were not accustomed to and thus fell under the strains of the regressed genetics.

And it should be noted, that the councils did not give off warnings soon enough, and many got infected before it became general knowledge. Another reason why the 6-12 pillar humans circumvented the councils, when they transferred to another system. The councils were too slow in their assessment of the dangers posed by the regressed races, and too eager to preserve the old genetic lineages. They still are.

cycle, we developed the new progression goals and programmed new code sheets to make a suitable energy system as well as selected the energies for the organic vessel of the new cycle.

Thus, we know how to act appropriately to the incoming energies and we are to make use of our innate knowledge to match what the NGC brings about. We know how to adjust and how to upgrade to follow the changes of our system, as well as what to do when a cycle ends and a new one begins.

Our energy system is capable of detecting the changes in the sun[27] and in the resonance grids of our system. We know how to initiate the correct preparations for what is coming. All we have to do is to listen to our inner information and shed off everything that prevents us from doing the needed *transition* and *transformation* work. We must arrange our lives so we can follow the changes and learn how to *transcend* the local convulsions in the areas we live in, the energetic instability in other humans and the changes in our surroundings.

Our template can similarly initiate changes, because all advanced information systems have encoded a form of *interactive intelligence* to corroborate with its owner. It is part of the template program and code sheets, we made, so we always would get back to progress in the direction of our goals, if we got stuck or lost our way.

Therefore, our template holds different trigger systems to initiate the needed changes, if our organic vessel and current state of existence should not respond appropriately to the original template program and the goals of why we are in this system. But we have to listen to it.

---

[27] Which is why many countries suffer from a blocking of the sun. The new cycle of the sun, going into the higher density layers, will effectively initiate these settings in our template and with that, begin our transition process.

The Clearing of Older Timelines

When we were about to enter a new cycle in the progressive systems, we did the work of clearing out all energetic and genetic remnants of the past, and of all we had been in that and the previous cycles.

To accomplish that work, we travelled back in time by making our own cross-timeline programs to do so. Travelling back in time means to interact with specific timelines in previous cycles, by incorporating parts of our future self into an older organic version on the chosen timelines. The goal of all travelling back was to upgrade the individual and racial genetics in the timelines we did not complete acceptably.

The reason why progressive humans travel back in time is to clear out all failed attempts and timelines, so they can function properly in the upcoming cycle of manifestation. It is natural for progressive humans to go back and forth on timelines to alter them in order to become more productive. The goal of higher productivity was also the idea behind the chiasm. Through the chiasm, inserted into our template, we would be able to detect the failed attempts in the existing life and not having to wait until the completion of the cycle to do the clearing work. Timeline work is linked to the cycles, the holographic grids and probability fields of all systems.

All humans in progressive systems take responsibility for their past by ensuring that nothing is left behind that can affect the futures of all systems in an unproductive way. Whatever lingers on, and remain uncleared, will hold everyone back like an anchor stuck in the depths of the unknown. The old energies and genetics on past timelines need to be released to enable all to move on. Besides, timelines continue to exist as long as they contain viable genetics. Hence, the joint work of all progressive races, when a new cycle is up, is to clear out their genetics on all past timelines to close down that cycle.

The problem with the regressed races has been that they do not do what is asked of them and most of their dysfunctional timelines and genetics remain operational in the regressed worlds and systems. The regressed races choose not to move forward, but want to prolong the timeline event and its energies for as long as possible. It has become a way of existence for them to put a halt unto other human realities, and their time travel is not aimed at cleaning up the past timelines, but has the function of reinforcing the outdated timelines by inserting new replicated genetics along with duplicates and clones.

On top of the obsolete timeline issues and the attempt from the regressed to prevent the highest progression rate to be achieved in the progressive systems, keeping whole cycles stuck in older energies, the regressed races have as well hijacked and reengineered worlds in full, within the progressive human systems, and kept these locked in with infected and contaminated templates and energy systems run by defective developmental programs, driven by technologically artificial timelines.

Our system has been struggling with this after the higher version of earth fell into the hands of the inverted races. This happened as a result of several bad choices, done by the majority of humans in the 2-8 to 5-11 pillars during Atlantis, despite the agreed work to achieve the highest purity rate, the standards and the highest progression rate of the 6-12 pillar, which we all approved in the first projects.

And yet, not to forget
Other humans and other races are there to remind us of what we truly are and what we are made of by our interaction with them and how they respond to us. We are to follow the Principles, the Rules and the Laws in all interactions. Other humans and races are the way-showers to get back into ourselves, no matter what others hold. Good or ill.

On Selflessness

Being selfless in the appropriate way means to work for the highest good of the many, but not in a self-submissive or self-destructive way or by expecting anything back in return. We do all that we do without any ulterior motives, because we know, we are part of an interactive and interlinked reality. We are connected to each other, since our organic vessels and energy systems are made from the same energy and resonance fields. What we do affect the collective human fields.

And consciousness is also interconnected, since it all sprung from the highest domains. Consequently, the foundation of all that we are is unified as well. Consciousness develop through energy in worlds and reality fields with lifeforms that act in an interdependent way. It was constructed this way to ensure the highest progression rate for all human races in all evolutionary cycles. This means, as we progress, so does our world. As our world progresses, so do we. Both above and below are we made of unified fields of consciousness and energy.

Conversely, if we regress, so does our world and all around us.

This does not make us into a unified whole[28] but it does make us fully responsible for the joint progression of our race and our world. All that we are - above, below, inside and outside - affect everything else. What we do, equally affect the resonance fields because every action is a potential use of reality energy on some level. Thus, how we utilize the energies of our reality, affects all (and thus the Laws).

Because of this, everything we are and do have to be in balance with the energies and the lifeforms in our reality to achieve harmony. *Harmony* arises on all levels of reality, when the highest good of the many is accomplished and not just what is good for us.

---

[28] As in we are all one, ref. the Law of One, which is technically a hive-mind mentality induced into the human collective by the RA Confederation aka the Blue Avians. A mindset the crystalline Sirians have adapted too. It ensures that their I-cubes work in the correct manner on all templates. The Blue Avians are part of the crystalline races.

Progression can only unfold when there is harmony. Harmony arises from the higher order capacities and knowledge of how to develop the energies in us and around us, in concurrence with the Natural Laws of Energetic Utilization. All forms of distortion arise from disharmony and the wrongful use of energy. Order, balance and harmony are thus key in the progressive worlds to ensure pure energies for all.

Higher order energy progresses within the realms of higher order and purified energies and distorted energies within the realms of impurity and distortion. This is the Law of Energetic Affinity.

Pure energy can only transform distorted energy, when the properties of the distorted energy are met with the proper counter-procedures. Being light, compassionate or all good[29] does not transform distortion and the regressed genetics; it pushes both into the hidden layers of our energy system, holding resonance for this, from earlier timelines beyond our current awareness.

Only the trained skills and the accurate knowledge of how to do the complete template clearing work and the willing approach to work with energy, will clear out all impurities. We are to relearn how to use our skills of transformation, transition and transcendence to get rid of all darkness and distortion.

Let us not repeat the mistakes of the past.

---

[29] That is, believing to be this, since these concepts are a deception. The properties of light and darkness were part of the false teachings of Atlantis. Back then, many chose to use the regressed rules of polarization and shy away from the impurities in them but in that, they made it possible for entities to possess them, since half of their energy system remained unaccounted for. Instead, they should have fought harder to clear out their impurities and not turned the blind eye to what they had become.

Reality Governance & The Third Pillar

In pillar 3-9, we learned how to apply the Natural Laws of Energetic Utilization into our progression work.

The Natural Laws administer the accurate use of the diverse forms of energy a world is composed of. This includes the Rules of Engagement to ensure the appropriate energetic exchange in all interaction in any inter-racial behavior, since every and all interactions are an exchange of information, energy and consciousness and thus a utilization of reality energy or human energy. How to do this in the accurate ways were merged into all progressive developmental programs.

The inter-racial communication and interaction programs from the 2-8 pillar work[30] were combined with the 3-9 pillar developmental work *with the detailed use of reality energy and human energy*, given that both centered around how to progress as part of a community, or within a group of humans, and how to perform creational projects that supported the furtherment of that group within a segment of reality.

    After completing the 2-8 programs and their cross-programs into the community work, the next stages of the progression work were exclusively within the 3-9 pillar, where the main focus was on how to manage the governance programs administering our reality field, how to adjust the grids and how to maintain the resonance fields.

---

[30] Each reality field has its own racial differences and thus dissimilar ways of behaving and being around each other. Diplomatic assessment and learning suitable ways of acting, when visiting another world, were part of the 2-8 pillar work.

When we had completed this, the developmental work went into the systemic progression work in the 4-10 pillar, where we learned how to work with our solar system and how to corroborate with the other solar systems and their core technologies.

Finally, before the 6-12 pillar work, we learned the programming and coding work of the developmental programs, the engineering of the technologies behind the reality and developmental programs etc. All of which were part of the 5-11 pillar work.

Reality Governance in Progressive Systems
Politics in progressive realities concern the best possible way to honor all expressions of life and how to achieve optimal utilization of the lifeforce, unfolded into organic vessels, by the usage of the finest possible genetic engineering – to continue the lineage of that system – as well as the most optimal utilization of energy and consciousness to develop and progress all organic lifeforms to unfold their highest consciousness potentials. This is achieved by using the developmental programs and accommodating technologies, such as the HTS.

Governance in all progressive systems runs automatically due to a broad chosen collection of developmental programs that uphold and run the societal structures governing any reality. The selection of the developmental programs is done by the majority in that world.

The collection of programs is overseen by *an advisory board* and it is a general choice to follow the recommendations of the advisory board of that system. The advisory board is a subsection of the higher order councils and they are in each world to ensure the highest purity rate, the highest standards and the highest progression rate for all of the races in that world as part of the overall system.

The advisory board upholds the recommendations from the core domains, and not just the progression rate of one system. The goal of all realities is to match the progression rate of all the pillars, because the pillar work defines the achievements of the systemic evolutionary cycles. Thus, reality governance is not something that is of individual concern in elections and political games, but a collective matter that is agreed upon by all members of that race within cyclic assemblies, where anyone can show up and decide for the upcoming minor cycle (a minor cycle is a specific level of energy to be developed) what will be the most optimal governance of that reality field and its resources. All is decided with the goal of matching the incoming energies of the upcoming and next cycles, along with the dynamics these have in the universal systems and how they will affect the various realities.

Once these agreements are in place – always a long debate - they are converted into developmental programs to produce the proper energetic settings of that reality, to ensure the highest standards etc. And then all will work for that goal. The choices and challenges are, of course, if all citizens want to follow the accepted standards or will choose another setting.

All progressive systems are based upon free will and diversity is acknowledged within the progression worlds. Nobody is forced to follow the collective settings, but if alternate choices of existence are chosen in a personal project, the segment that is developed and explored under that project must follow the overall Principles, Rules and Laws of that reality. Otherwise it serves no purpose or function and it is considered disruptive for the common goal of all. The project is considered failed and must be terminated immediately and a more productive project must be initiated instead, showing good will and the wish to be of the highest service for the whole.

Therefore, the only way a race can override the Principles, Rules and Laws of a system, is if it deliberately tampers with the facilities and changes its developmental programs. All systems and their core facilities in regressed systems have been tampered with.

Relative Reality & Segregation Dynamics

In our transition work, to match the incoming extra-systemic energies and the subsequent energetic upgrading that is possible, if we work with the cycles of the NGC, the dynamics of relative reality becomes important. The possibility of creating a relative reality around us to match our genetics and energy system, and what we want to achieve with our progression work, originate from the progressive worlds.

Relative reality is based upon the idea that if any member of a race chooses to work outside the collectively accepted standards, to ensure diversity, that member is allowed to develop a new segment.

But if that member chooses not to work for the highest good of the many defined by the standards, i.e. the Principles, Rules and Laws of that reality, that member will eventually be - by the choices and the energies created in the self-made segment – transferred to a reality more suitable for that preferred kind of consciousness, energy and ways of living. These are the segregation dynamics and the dynamics behind the different zones of reality.

The relative reality possibility and the segregation dynamics are still at work in our system, since the original construction remained part of the progressive segment of our system, in spite of the hijacking. The original construction was secured before the takeover.

This fact, that the core facilities of our reality are intact, is behind the extensive tampering with the collective human consciousness field to shut down any innate knowledge, followed up by incorrect teachings, diminished sciences and belief systems to create regressed energies and standards within the lower order human world, we call Earth. However, it is important to notice to following:

If we do not like what we participate in, in our world, we can recreate our energy system and enable it to follow the Principles, Rules and Laws in accord with the progressive worlds. If we chose to do so, we generate an energy and consciousness segment to our liking in our current world and in that segment, we can unfold our choices and consciousness from which we can prepare the next organic vessel and what type of world, we want to be part of – if not in this solar system then in another.

In the transition work, we build our personal segment and then we can enter into e.g. the rehabilitation zones, where things will work in our favor, if we follow the Principles, Rules and Laws. The guidelines support our endeavors to get back on track with the progression standards. But first we have to get to a higher order energetic state, where we can detach from the base program in the personal clearing and rebuilding work.

A progressive human wants to achieve the highest level of his or her being and at the same time do what is considered the highest good of the many – including clearing out and remove what cannot prosper into the highest purity rate, the highest standards and the highest progression rate.

Progressive humans choose to progress to gain more knowledge and to develop all realities to their highest potentials[31] by the use of their knowledge.

Progressive humans do not continue to feed energy to what has failed or what should be shut down, if it leads to unfortunate futures.

The shutting down of failed projects prevents the domino effect of a possibility to turn into a probability. By cleaning up all energies in the project, when the possibility of a prospected failure gets too strong, the manifestation of the failed is avoided.

In that way we preserve the reality fields in their best condition and our energy system along with it. Any failure, we have maintained, will become part of the energies that pull us down and into the regressed spiral, because they create disharmony and distortion.

---

[31] Contrary to the regressed races that want to pull everything down to where they are in the failed worlds and within the reversed systems.

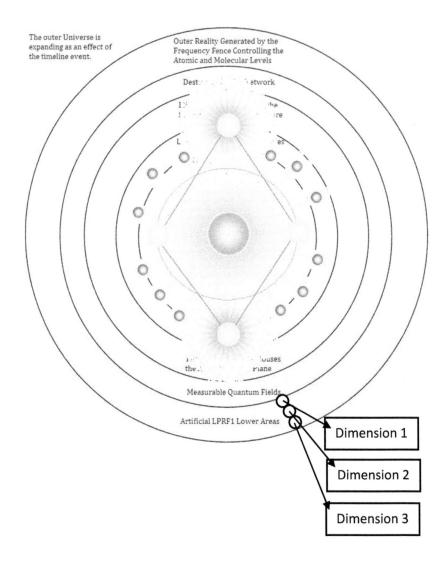

The outer Universe is
expanding as an effect of
the timeline event.

Outer Reality Generated by the
Frequency Fence Controlling the
Atomic and Molecular Levels

Dest........ etwork

Measurable Quantum Fields

Artificial LPRF1 Lower Areas

Dimension 1

Dimension 2

Dimension 3

The Challenges of the Councils

Remarks on No Interference
To throw it in there and to shut down the false belief system that the directive of no interference, as taught in the Star Trek movies, apply to our solar system or any system at all.

There is no such thing as no interference in matters that concern the progression of life, consciousness and the utilization of energy in worlds that are interconnected. Progression of any race, concerns all races, because we are a humongous united system of consciousness, energy and life. What happens in one system affects all systems.

If one race fails, it affects all the other races stemming from the same genetic root and its subsequent human lineages. Genetics are interconnected. All worlds and reality fields are interconnected. And thus, all races work together to ensure the highest progression rate for all.

No Aliens Either
Secondly, we need to grasp that there are no extraterrestrial races, as in opposition to the human races as most understands it. As in we are the earth humans and the aliens or extraterrestrials are another class of humanoid or human races, different from ours.

We all stem from one large group of 12 original universal human races and the lineages that sprung from them. Some of these original humans turned regressed because of their own choices and in that developed into the humanoid races. Other human lineages continued to progress as part of the original 12 universal lineages, i.e. the true human races. The 12 universal human races came from a preceding cycle, from other forms of existence and entered into our universe to continue their progression journey, using the advanced constructions made by the Ancient Ones. The Ancient Ones were a highly advanced human race, which in their cycles developed the many universes we are part of.

Our Own Mess

Thirdly, the human race is not a developing race to be overseen and mentored by other races. Consequently, because of our ancestry and composition, we cannot write of the responsibilities of our old actions and choices, which have led to the position we are in today. A highly advanced race can only be hijacked if the circumstances allow for it.

A long time ago humans accepted the hijacking, when humanity – as the advanced race it was - could have said no and fought against it. Always remember that. Bad choices were made and we are forced to repeat these choices over and over again, until we learn to make the correct ones, following the true progression dynamics.

There are no victims in the mess, we are part of. There is only the absence of responsibility and the nonexistence of the overall will to take the appropriate actions, when it was called for and it still is so. We have to accept these conditions and then choose to do something about it. On a big scale.

Thus, humanity in our system has heaps to learn, compared to other similar races controlled by the regressed races. In many ways our race, due to its initial position in the overall work towards the 6th dimension, has been kept in the dark to prevent the first human race, that chose to work this way, to complete the 6-12 pillar work into the next cyclic setup. Because if one human race could do it, other human races could too. Luckily, other progressive humans have completed the work in adjacent systems. It has no purpose for the regressed to keep us in the pit anymore. Or so it might seem. The future will tell.

The Challenges of the Councils – Historically
In our system the political issues, which began in Atlantis, were to be resolved in the progressive councils dealing with the bigger picture of the problems that arose from the timeline event.

The human races progress within complex higher order systems built of advanced technologies. Everyone is progressing within the sciences of how to develop life, consciousness and energy and with that, the best ways of keeping all on track. A continued work for all involved.

Because of this, any chosen change has to be for the highest good of the many and not just to solve a crisis in one minor solar system that, in its construction and situation, is similar to other human systems having suffered under the regressed, reverted and inverted races. The culprit of the anti-progressive races extends far beyond our system, due to their halting of many similar systems.

The process of freeing our system was never simple and it is far from completed. It has been, in the higher order worlds, a political hot potato and lots of pieces have to come together to solve the bigger picture of our system and the systems connected to ours. It must be remembered that all strategies for progression are incomprehensible for most humans, having little or no considerations of how universes and their races are progressed and evolved.

The first political issues were focused on how to restore the old genetic lineages, dating back to Lemuria and Atlantis, although for now trapped in 4th dimensional dysfunctional organic vessels under the 4-10 pillar. Part of that issue was how to reboot our solar system and upgrade the ancient lineages to make these and humanity able to get back into the progressive developmental programs and allow the technologies, part of the original constructions, to work according to the universal progression standards. Consequently, the problems at that time revolved around the issues of the continuation of the old races, of how to develop these lineages, despite their dire state.

The other half of the issue was how to preserve the old genetics within humanity and find a way to upgrade their lower fields within the generated developmental programs, created and administered by the adjacent reality human and humanoid races aka the Settlers.

After the failure of Atlantis, everyone with viable genetics had been transferred into new organic vessels within new communities as part of an agreed reseeding. These last human projects, under the timeline event energetic settings, were administered by the Settlers, i.e. the overseeing Pleiadians, the here-living mammal-avian Sirian As and the White Orion humans amongst others, along with groups of humanoid races choosing to stay here.

The higher order councils trusted the here-living races and thought they were working for an acceptable solution, benefitting the highest good of the many and were working for a progression out of the LPU settings. These races had promised to fall back in line after their failed projects in Atlantis. The councils believed the information given by the Settlers and assumed our system was moving in a progressive direction for all involved. That is, solutions benefitting the ancient human lineages, the old here-living human and humanoid races from other systems and humanity.

Unfortunately, these races played a strategic double game with the councils, giving them false information and hence the councils did not have the complete picture of what was really going on here.

Aside from the absence of accurate information from the here-living races, the councils were also being manipulated by infiltrators residing within the councils. The infiltrators dragged all decisions into the infinite of no-solutions. Both within our solar system and outside. The infiltrators made sure nothing changed that could shut down the allowances of the here-living races. Hence, the nonappearance of any intervention and actions in our system over the first several thousand years after the failure of Atlantis.

The Challenges of the Councils in 2020 and Onward
All human races are to progress into the 6-12 pillar, once they have completed the preceding pillars. The progression work is built up of developmental processes and normally the amount of progressions needed for this, are granted within the different cycles.

But because of the NGC and the alteration of all universes, new issues are pressuring the councils. One of the new issues is how to avoid a complete destruction of the existing reality fields, of which many are behind schedule in the initial pillar programs. Because, as the NGC comes in, everybody must follow the pull or choose not to and if so, be put under extinction protocol within segregated realities. Thus, lots to be taken into consideration.

Another issue the councils revolve around, is how to develop the original genetics here and in other systems into a strain holding no possibility for regression in any of the future universal lineages – and perhaps use our system as a blueprint of how to do so, but in that allowing for new issues to be dealt with here.

At the same time the main concern has developed into a wide-ranging consideration of how to preserve the original construction in our system and at the same time assist humanity in an upgrading.

Along with the actions to be taken to get the remaining regressed races to leave and how to ensure they cannot return.

Finally, the case of the Settlers and their transgressions within our system has become an issue too and whether they are to stand trial or are just asked to leave. Actions are needed in this matter, because the Settlers have been allowing for extra-systemic interference which has not been, and is not, for the highest good of the many.

To accommodate for this, the councils have agreed on closing down all ancient 4th cycle projects under the Settlers as well as a complete removal from the Library of the templates used in the LPU programs, together with annulling their developmental projects. Projects, which have been favoring the Settlers and allowed for a continuation of their businesses here. This agreement will shut down all prerogatives and allowances the Settlers might have here, along with their operating vessels within the human population. In essence, a total exclusion of their reason to be here. If they choose to stay, it will be to show good will and to do the same work as humanity; i.e. to get ready for the last two stages of the NGC as it reaches and activates the 2-8 racial grid and racial networks in 2026-2034, and the succeeding 1-7 individual activation and cleanup cycle. And then, a return to the true ways.

Nevertheless, the grand scale knots and bolts of the continuation of the human race, its template and technological challenges and the futures of the human race, are up to the councils to solve and what they choose of proceedings to ensure any furtherment of humanity.

However, on a systemic level, things are already in motion because of the new grand cycle. And if the old councils cannot solve the issues of the future, the new grand cycle and the completed 6-12 human races will.

Let us go back in time to understand the bad choices made by a minority of the ancient humans and the circumstances behind.

The Bad Choices of the Minority

Before we move into the explanations on this, let us not forget that in the new pillar systems the human races had experienced nothing but worlds with order, balance and harmony, and suddenly all changed into chaos and destruction around them. The pillar humans were not equipped to handle the effects of the blast from the timeline event and what the energies had been imbued with, as these spread into the foundation and the grids of the pillars.

To Recapture

The 3rd cycle failed in every way and it was this warring, technological driven cycle that pushed a group of humans to address the Ancient Ones and obtained the allowances to start all over again here. Human races from accompanying cycles agreed to participate in the project, starting afresh in a brand new 4th cycle with the new type of organic vessels. Most of what had played out were erased from all timelines and did not become part of the knowledge base in the new vessels or the new worlds. Although complete records of the past were stored in the racial Library including a protype of the old organic vessels and templates – along with the 12 Primes. All were to begin anew, even though many of the participants chose to position an organic version of themselves in stasis pods, outside the newly created systems.[32]

---

[32] The timeline event took most of these pods out. Some have remained, but as long as there are timeline event remnants in our system, it is impossible to retrieve these pods. If all could agree on letting go of the ATE worlds, transform all DE1 levels and upgrade all DE2 and DE3 to their correct BTE settings, it would be possible via the records, the genetic samples and the templates stored in the Library, to recreate the original BTE organic vessels both pre-pillar and first pillar humans.

The idea behind the pillar worlds and systems was to complete the remaining cycles by the means of human consciousness, respectful use of reality energy and by honoring life to avoid what had played out in the 3rd cycle. To ensure that no group would turn against each other, as they did in the 3rd cycle, the pillar systems were constructed of various triune reality fields with an outer domain, a middle domain and a core domain as an interconnected whole, where every citizen took part in the joint progression dynamics etc. as explained earlier. The inner domain was associated with the core domain and these two levels administered the maintenance of the original facilities, and if needed, upgrades of the systemic constructions.

The timeline event began in the Sirian Workstations due to wrongful use of grid energy in an unfortunate experiment to engineer further holographic spaces within spaces by harnessing the 3rd cycle energies. Something went wrong and what could have been an expansion into new living spaces, became an inversion of energy and a reversal of the Sirian grids into partial 3rd cycle, partial 5th cycle energies, but now in a distorted way, which also affected the Sirian technology.

After the inverted energies[33] had changed the Sirian resonance fields they rippled outwards into the other density systems, altering these as well. The 2-8 pillar, 3-9 pillar, 4-10 pillar and 5-11 pillar humans got infused with 3rd cycle energies, by the means of the racial networks, which now had been imbued with genetic fragments from the ancient failed human projects that had been left behind in the wasted fields of the 3rd cycle.[34]

---

[33] Instead of radiating and vibrating energy, inverted holographic entities and organic humans suck out energy and genetics from other lifeforms to sustain themselves.

[34] In the old worlds it was normal procedure to push genetic remnants from failed human projects into pockets of enclosed energy in deep space (old cyclic energy), where they could burn out. All of this will be cleared during the NGC.

Now to the Choices

So, what were the unfortunately choices done by a minority of the progressive humans that altered the course of history for us all?

It was complicated circumstances ATE, and lots of mistakes were made. Situations beyond imagination popped up here and there, and everyone tried to manage the new settings. However, at the end of the day, it all came down to disagreements that arose as the reality fields began to crumble and drop, and every attempt to preserve the human lineages seemed to end in failure. Numerous trials and errors were made to fix the situation, but nothing seemed to work.

Fortunately, most of the ATE proceedings and horrible events are lost in the past and should remain hidden, but some of the errors are still affecting us to this day and thus they will be addressed here.

The inner domains got hit by the infection first, followed by similar events in the Ursa Major system, the Pleiadian and the Sirian systems (one of the large other-systemic triangles connected to our system), and the humans in the outer and middle domains did what they could to keep their resonance fields, holographic grids and racial networks safe by constructing repulsion barriers between the infected realities and the non-infected realities.

Everyone tried – for a very long time – to solve the issues with the infected genetics and the worlds that arose from the timeline event, but no viable solutions came up.

It was so, because the composition of the infection was beyond comprehension and none of the advanced genetic engineering could match the infected genetics. Solutions that came up would fit one layer of the code sequences in the infection but not all of them, given that the energies fueling the infected genetics were a mix of outdated 3rd cycle energies and pillar reality 5th cycle energies, creating a newfangled form of hybrid code sequences.[35] The only feasible solution was to remove the 5th cycle energies from the genetics and leave the 3rd cycle failed genetics to evaporate, as they were bereft of any fuel. And yet, that solution would mean a total quarantine of the infected humans within their worlds, plus a transfer of the healthy racial grids to the non-infected areas, as well as leaving behind the infected grids. What would occur from that was unpredictable.

However, a minority of the pillar humans did not agree with the proposed solution. Mostly, because they found it difficult to refrain from any further contact with their infected group members, in spite of the bigger picture of keeping the non-infected areas safe, and they continued to travel to the infected realities in an attempt to solve the energetic and genetic issues. They felt that if they knew more, they would find a cure.

A pillar group is theoretically a sub-group of the root races consisting of the same type of racial genetics, having similar genetic traits and often on the same developmental level in the pillar work. Such groups are interconnected and grow as a community of individuals working together to progress as a whole. A pillar group is also called a lineage.

The Origin of the Regressed Races

In some of the other-systemic realities, less hit by the timeline event, the there-living humans had stopped the infection, but they could not restore completely. They had cut away several code sequences from their template to clear the infection. Unfortunately, the incomplete

---

[35] The polarity arose from the double code sequences, holding inverted energy and viable energy. All infected humans got the double code system. Part of them looked viable and normal, and then within a hidden section of the template, the 3rd cycle inverted energy would create an alter ego out of the imbued genetics. This polarity – which still exist - is difficult to detect for most humans. Only humans dating back to BTE can see the old forms of energy and the infected genetics in the template.

template began to dematerialize and a breakdown of the remaining viable genetics then followed. Eventually, they managed to stop the genetic breakdown by recreating 3rd cycle reality cubes to keep their viable genetics intact.[36] Because of the altering of their template and the recoupling to the 3rd cycle technology, they stepped back in their evolutionary cycle. They knew the risks involved in this, but they had counted on figuring out how to re-evolve and mend later on, when the infection was more under control. Instead, they turned into what we know as the regressed humanoid races.

Nonetheless, most of the humanoids accepted what had unfolded and they came to terms with the transformed settings and their new organic vessels that had changed appearance to match the remaining genetics. They re-engineered their worlds, along with generating new laws and dynamics to pause the regression dynamics. Their laws and dynamics took form as a reversed version of the progression laws and dynamics to suit the reversed reality settings, they had come to exist under. They could do so, because as they removed sections of their template and their organic vessel transformed into a new being, they were pushed outside the progressive worlds due to the segregation dynamics. They were no longer part of the universal human lineages, and thus answered to no one.[37] With this newly obtained autonomy from the agreements of the progressive worlds, they chose to focus on an upgraded version of the 3rd cycle technologies and took on the

---

[36] Reality cubes were widely used in the 3rd cycle worlds. Via these cubes, realities and their humans would be infused with identical genetic sequences and their energy systems would be locked-in with the same energetic coding. Diversity and free will were not an option back then.

[37] The Taurians (from the constellation Taurus) still have their Prime in the Library and they could, if they would change their ways, become a progressive human again. The same goes with some of the other regressed races. The constellations around us are the old human worlds that regressed into insectoid, avian, reptoid or mammal races and regressed worlds. BTE we could shift between the reality fields. The timeline event caused the gaps between the worlds.

identity as trade nations. As it turned out, they adapted and found the reversed cycle useful. It was very similar to the 3rd cycle worlds.[38] For them, the reversed possibility had opened up to timelines in older evolutionary cycles and long forgotten parallel universes, where they found other older races to ally with, and trade became their survival.

The Trickery

A delegation of humans, from the minority group, travelled to the regressed humanoids to examine if the regressed would share what they had learned of the ATE genetic structure and how they managed to undo the infection, as well as how they had stopped the breaking down of their genetics. Sharing of knowledge between the regressed races and this group of pillar humans became a fact. However, it was a sharing that went further than any had anticipated. Mainly because the humans trusted the humanoids, and they thought the humanoids were still honoring the progressive laws and the rules of engagement. This was not the case, and the longer the human group stayed in the regressed worlds, the more the regressed humanoids wanted what the progressive humans had, i.e. viable and non-infected genetics. The progressive humans reminded them of all they had been before the reversal.

In the end of it all, the human group got tricked by the regressed races and subsequently modified. In captivity, they were infused with infected humanoid genetics in experiments done by the regressed to see if the human energy system could restore the humanoid genetics. That was not the case either.

Instead, the regressed learned that the progressive humans were able to produce genetics, and it was possible to inject their healthy genetics into the humanoid energy system. From the injections with

---

[38] Of course, we can speculate if that was not the ultimate goal of the experiment in the Sirian Workstations, i.e. to dismantle the pillar project and return to the old ways.

the pillar human genetics, their regression could be kept status quo, without having to be linked up to an I-cube. Following this discovery, new foul plans were molded and brewed. The possibility of trading the viable genetics to other races in the parallel universes were right there in front of them, and the regressed decided to turn the non-infected humans into tools to get access to the non-infected realities.

Once the regressed had altered the humans, turning them more humanoid in energy and consciousness than pillar human, they were returned to their own worlds in unmanned crafts, in stasis pods.

This delegation was turned into a trojan horse, literally. As they woke up, they slowly infiltrated the non-infected worlds on all levels and eventually, they sold out everything to the regressed. What was good-intended people trying to fix a big problem for all, became the entranceway into the Workstations and the non-infected reality fields and they handed it all into the hands of the regressed.

The Fall of the Pleiadian System
The Pleiadians succeeded in their work with the genetic modification, using *transformation* and *transcendence* to withstand the remains of the infection of their system. The Pleiadians had a scientific approach to things, and they chose to segregate the most infected humans in their system, and then altered the energetic settings of their reality fields. They transformed all grids and modified the racial network to hold edited versions of the original genetic markers. In essence, they created a whole new system where they transcended all the original pillar settings, but still within the agreed arrangements of the pillar project and the 12 universal human lineages.

Unfortunately, they were later on eradicated in the subsequent Orion-Pleiadian Wars, where the involved Pleiadians got captured and turned into something horrible in the Orion system. The trojan horse method was used there as well to get access to the fully safe-guarded

Pleiadian system. A very small portion of Pleiadians escaped to the Sirian A system, but were sold out by the Sirian As that had joined the White Orions. The majority of the Pleiadian lineages are today part of the regressed races, modified in different hybrid programs. They look Pleiadian, but they are more reptoid and avian than human.

The Fall of the Sirian System
The Sirians, within what was left of the non-infected grids, tried the approach of *transformation* and *transition*, but did not manage well. Their idea was to use the 3rd cycle energies – as they wanted to begin with, hence the initial experiment that led to the timeline event – and transform the old energy units by the means of the 5th cycle energy. In essence, uplift the old by the use of the new. But old is old, and new is new and should not be amalgamated.[39] Mostly because the 3rd cycle existed outside the pillar project and the 5th cycle was within. In all what they did, it seemed as if they persistently wanted to revive the 3rd cycle within the progressive worlds.

Along with these experiments, they continued the utilization of their holographic technologies in their attempts to modify the genetic lineages, in spite of the timeline event energies that had affected all their technologies, along with infecting the interactive consciousness units in their holographic programs.

Their genetic work was factually based upon infected holographic programs and 3rd cycle polluted technologies, and this dysfunctional modification lead to the occurrence of the inverted Sirian-Orion races and consequently to the crystalline technology, as an attempt to fix

---

[39] The old cannot be "ascended" by transformation, i.e. the process of upgrading all older forms of consciousness units, infusing them with new cyclic energies. There is a reason why the cycles are left behind. The only approach is to delete and evaporate the old. Something old has to go for something new to come in. Letting go has always been difficult for the Sirians.

that mistake. The crystalline technology isolates the infected genetics in the template, but it does not repair the genetics and eventually the infection breach through. They should have let it all go and started anew. However, due to this rigidity and need to preserve the old, the majority of the Sirian B lineages fell one by one.

A large group of the Sirian B races went to the Andromeda system (M31), where they continued as a semi-crystalline race, continuing their attempts to right the wrongs they had done. What remains of these Sirian B lineages are today either crystalline or android. Some of them merged with the Andromedas, turning into a new race.

The non-regressed Sirian As were finally taken over by the White Orion lineages, which – for the sake of survival in their own system – had shifted into the humanoid Orion agenda. A group from the White Orion-Sirian A humanoid lineages entered our system, during the Neolithic era, attempting to survive here by becoming the Settlers.

The Two Methods
In the *transforming* and *transcending* method, the timelines, genetics and technologies are cleared of their old cyclic energies to let what cannot uphold itself, evaporate and cease to be. Then what is left of viable energies and genetics are reactivated. Given the holographic properties, the viable genetics and energies can be recreated into a new template and energy system using the code sheets. However, to avoid a reconnection to the old energies and consciousness units in overlooked timelines etc. creating the possibility for a relapse, *the new template and energy systems are altered into a slightly different version*. As what was done in the pillar project.

The correct method of *transformation* and *transition*, is to activate and transform the infected or polluted genetics by restoring them to their original setting. If they are viable, they can stand on their own and continue within the now cleared energy system and template. *The goal is to keep the original energy system and let that continue.* If not, the genetics will evaporate following the activation and cleanup. The template will retract to the Library. Then, the overall grids and reality fields can recalibrate to their original pillar or pre-pillar settings on their own, because there are no lifeforms keeping the out-of-date energy and genetics in circulation.[40] Everything will transition into the purified and correct reality settings, and then a reseeding can take place of the original templates etc. Similar to the dynamics of the NGC.

Both methods were developed as a reaction to the wrongful use of energy and genetics in the 3rd cycle.

The Intra-systemic Lineages

Many of the humans from our system that got captured, or chose to shift side, are either part of the human population today or living in adjacent highly advanced realities. The first group of these human live inside our reality, in a fully sealed-off state, and they are unaware of their choices that led to our demise. Most of these are part of the ones that regretted later on and tried to change what had happened. They were taken out by their own.

The second group became active members of "the powers that be", knowing what they did, but having achieved power positions via their collaboration with the regressed races. This group live in other-dimensional reality settings next door to our world from where they run the world show, in which humanity is seen as mere production units. Their priority is to preserve their power positions and keep the

---

[40] One of the main reasons for the overpopulation. Since each human hold less viable genetics, other lifeforms have been engineered and injected with smaller fragments than what is needed to make a human function correctly.

wheels running in the setup, they have arranged for themselves. They have no interest in changes, because – as in the case of the Settlers – they will have to stand trial for everything they have done under the rulership of the regressed. They are called the intra-systemic human lineages.

It cannot be disputed that the bad choices of this minority led to a continuation of something that could have ended eons ago. Either because they were taken out and accepted the penalty of that in a sort of self-punishment, not fighting the sealing off,[41] or because they became part of the power factions under the regressed. Both moves led to a fueling of what were on the brink of dying out.

It was agreed on, in the Workstations, to take the approach of segregation and transcension, similar to what the Pleiadians did. And if this minority had stayed within the repulsion barrier and followed the general agreements, the infected and regressed systems would have burned out a long time ago due to lack of viable genetics and energy, or changed so profoundly that they energetically would have been repelled by the progressive resonance fields and altogether segregated from our system, and pushed into a previous cycle. But instead this minority ensured the continuation of the infection and the timeline event within our system by their actions.

Today, the intra-systemic human lineages are still clinging on to their positions within the regressed races. They are preventing the highest good of the many to unfold in our system and they are a hindrance to be alleviated at some point, because they continually work to block the incoming energies and the winds of change.

---

[41] Which is ridiculous. They had all the means to make everything right, if only they had fought harder. Nothing was corrected by accepting the sealing off because in that, they become the first of many and allowed for a sealing off in general. They continued to make the wrong choices.

Eventually, the intra-systemic lineages will run out of energy and their work will be shut down as the regressed races take off. They will join the SSN in the dying cold DE1 universe later into the future. Most of them already have, teaming up to find genetic solutions for their non-continuance. However, it does not take away the current resistance from the intra-systemic lineages and their constant attempt to halt the mandatory progression of humanity. It would be easy, if we were only fighting the regressed races, but in fact, we also have our own race to deal with. Both within the current world setup and outside in the next-door worlds belonging to the intra-systemic human lineages. Let us not forget that. Humans are not just humans.

The Moon – the Big Cube

One of the big pieces of technology, allowed into our system by the intra-systemic lineages, is the moon. The intra-systemics allowed, late in the stages of Atlantis as it had begun its downfall, fugitives from an old 3rd cycle system into our solar system. The fugitives original name has been forgotten, but we can refer to them as the lunar races. They were completely alien to our solar system, and their evolutions failed along with the rest of the 3rd cycle.

The first thing they did at arrival was to insert an artificial sphere, on which they lived for a while, but as they drained the sphere of all resources, as the 3rd cycle races had as a depraved habit, they had to move and the only next step was to become part of our reality.

The planetoid was reconstructed and turned into a huge spherical I-cube. With this, they coded segments of our grid, racial network and reality energies to enable them to exist here. From the inserted lunar programs, energy imprints and code systems, the lunars created their new human vessels. And of course, they kept a door open back into their old worlds. Thus, the moon functions as a coding I-cube and as a bridge into the failed lunar worlds with their humanoid versions and lots of androids.[42] Quite a lot of the hostile androids, we have been dealing with in our system, have used the moon to access our system.

The main function of the moon is to adjust the holographic grids and racial network to the timeline event energies and the parallel worlds, still using these energies as a foundation of their grids. It also ensures a circulation of the timeline event energies (old 3rd cycle and distorted Sirian 5th cycle) into our section of the solar system. This is amplified by larger coding cubes positioned in the parallel worlds, making the moon emit large portions of ancient cyclic energies.[43]

The moon functions as a massive 3rd cycle cube, controlling the coding of the electrochemical molecules in the lunar humans, along with the code systems that produce their bio-fields, their emotional fields and their mental fields. The lunar races, although looking human, are still alien to our system since their human vessels and energy systems are distinctively 3rd cycle. The energies, they emit, are also 3rd cycle.

Many of the lunar humans have made high positions for themselves inside our world, dating back to ancient Egypt and Mesopotamia, as well as within the ancient high cultures of South America. All ancient cultures worshipping the moon, had lunar humans as their priesthood, kings or tribal leaders.

The main objective of the lunar races, inside our world, is to keep the global human racial network connected to the lunar cube. As long as the lunar humans are in our world as a race, the moon will remain its position.

---

[42] Another group of the lunars collaborated with the black Orions, a 3rd cycle race, and many of the lunar humanoids hold insectoid, avian and mammal genetics of a nasty Orion variant from the old evolutionary cycles – all are controlled by cubes.
[43] Technically, the frequency colors are the rainbow of these old energies.

The possibility for the lunars, if they want to progress with the rest of the ancient human races, is to change the code systems of the moon and close the back-door. Otherwise their planetoid and their grids will go down with the rest of the DE1 dying solar system.

If the moon was changed to hold progressive energies instead of regressive, it could bridge the renewed energy into their molecular structures and alter their energy systems. This would give them the appropriate foundation for their organic vessels and enable them to alter their fields into the original composition of the heart and brain fields. They would then turn into progressive humans.

This solution is being worked on and is a possibility. Naturally, the sciences behind a reconfiguration of the moon are discussed in the councils, as in how an alteration of the energetic composition of the moon would affect the gravitational pull of our planet[44] along with the effects on the orbital mechanics of the other planets in our solar system, in the transition period. While that debate is going on, the back-door into the parallel worlds are in the process of being closed and with that, the removal of the ancient lunar technologies, facilities and androids within our system. The long-needed recalibration of the progressive grids and racial networks belonging to the original solar system human lineages, are also in progress.

Making the Right Choices

It is important to understand that those of us who are aware today and choose the responsibilities of the progression work, we cannot support the intra-systemic lineages and their world setup. We cannot participate in their agreements with the regressed or lunar races, or

---

[44] The planet, we currently live on, is the timeline event equivalent of the original reality field. In the future dying DE1, there will be planets as we see it in the universe, but they will not hold any forms of life. The living grids and racial networks have been removed and transferred to the DE2 level.

give fuel to their orchestrated world show under these factions. We must create our own jurisdictions and make new ways of living.[45]

We cannot give energy to what preserves the timeline event, the DE1 settings and the powers that be, but work to do the transformation, the transition and the transcension, the best ways we can.

Because anyone that clings on to the current ways of being human, which in essence is similar in many ways to the old races of the failed 3rd cycle, becomes today's block-stopper of the incoming energies.

We must educate ourselves and do what we can to remember how to work with our template and the timelines connected to it, to be able to free us from the supremacy of the regressed, the lunars and the intra-systemic races, their timelines, their worlds and remove all their inserted genetics in us.

---

[45] Of course, we have to transform and transition out of the current world settings within what is possible (we still have to buy clothes, shoes etc.). But we will do that by minimizing our needs, by becoming a knowledgeable consumer and avoiding the regressed companies, their jurisdictions etc. We will learn to behave in ways that clearly state our non-participation. Ways for us to figure out in the upcoming years. Hence the-to-come HAL Educations, the HAL Business portal and the HAL Innovations to give ideas on how to transition into a new human within a new world setup.

The Big Choices

There are no easy solutions to the systemic challenges and they rest in the hands of the councils, as mentioned earlier, since most of the systemic challenges are beyond our control. However, we do have a huge impact on the individual challenges and the consequences are something we can work with, if we choose to do so. It begins with the choices of change, and how extensively we are ready to work for it.

To Recapture

The true composition of our solar system is highly advanced. It is just the segment, we live in, that has been kept low-leveled by the use of timeline event energies. For now, our solar system appears to consist of electromagnetic energies. And yet it does not; the moment we get our complete perception field and our higher order awareness back, the 4th dimensional prohibiting technologies and the adjacent reality fields, with their lifeforms, will appear.

Humans are to understand that the reality setup, they see, is a limited version showing merely half the picture. It is so because the human perception field has been tampered with. The normal human cognitive abilities are dysfunctional and underdeveloped, supported by a limited eye sight restricted within the spectrum of light, along with limited sensing and limited awareness faculties.

The quantum fields, all kinds of electromagnetic energy and the atoms are the remnants of the timeline event. This energetic setting is referred to as the density 1 fields. Although the density 1 is correct in the after-timeline-event reality constructions, it is incorrect in the before-timeline-event realities. There the lowest realities existed in density 2, i.e. from the 4th to 6th dimensions, which at the time was the density 1. The current DE1, i.e. from the 1st to 3rd dimensions, is an artificial construction and unnatural. Therefore, as the NGC does it work, the DE1 will activate its content, followed by an evaporation as the distorted 5th cycle Sirian energies fade out and what came from the 3rd cycle will cease to be. The DE1 and all that are built upon these energies are set to go, after which the DE2 becomes the lowest field of existence again.

The original solar system recovering dynamics are in the making, and then there is humanity situated in the lower order energy section. And what are humans to do, as their reality changes and huge sections are removed into the density 2, leaving behind a dying cold density 1?

The Big Choices
Humanity have to make the clear choices to leave behind their usage of outdated forms of energy and their archaic methods of utilization of the reality resources.

The climate changes can be of assistance to teach humanity a higher responsibility for their environment. Because as reality kicks back and shows humanity, how their ways of arranging themselves in this world have become unacceptable, perhaps more humans will be eager to do the right choices for a better future for all.

Humans have to change their ways of living, if they want a chance of a continuation of their existence. The future awaits the humans that are willing to do the transition into the progressive sections of our solar system, and the rest will meet the final stages of the NGC and the cleanup dynamics over the next 100 years or so. It is only possible to do a global transition for the entire human population and shifting our reality field in full, if a majority of humans choose to leave behind their present-day ways of living, and if they choose to return to the progressive lifestyle.

However, given the downsizing of most humans, that possibility is slim. But what can be set as a goal for humanity as a whole, is that all humans must learn to regard all lifeforms with respect, since we are genetically built from similar forms of DNA and energies.

The common man and woman must integrate four simple steps and live by them in their everyday lives, to continue a tolerable existence as the NGC does its work. The steps have been taught in all ancient cultures, given that the information about the NGC was initially given some 2550 years ago:

1. Becoming herbivore or frugivore.
2. Have mutual respect for all lifeforms.
3. Start following the cultural laws to the dot – no cheating, no stealing and no twisting of cultural moral, out of self-interest.
4. Taking self-responsibility for advanced learning, either as part of the education system or by the means of the free material on the Internet, doing self-education.

We cannot expect other people to do the progression work.

However, those of us that choose to do the progression work, we can do the transition and the needed transformation, and in that create a bigger possibility for more to follow. We will become the role models and the first of many.

And that will take us to the individual challenges and what we can do to meet up with the transition energies.

The Individual Challenges

The individual challenges involve the work with the lower order fields and how we can clear these to get to the point, where we can rebuild our higher order constitution. As long as we are trotting along in our human form, exercising our human will, mind and emotions, we will not get to the higher order levels in us. The higher order levels of us contain the consciousness genetics, the original template and higher order energy system. These parts have been hidden from us. We are to figure out how to reconnect to the true parts of us and then put in the needed work to activate them.

Before we begin the bigger work, we need to arrange our everyday life to make room for the transition work. It is not possible to go on with business as usual, if we truly want to progress. The everyday life must change, because it is partaking in the distortion programs. Our choices must reflect the Principles, the Rules and the Laws and it is a given that we cannot sit on both chairs in this work. We must choose our reality setting. Either we are part of the base program and the normal human life, or we live according to the higher awareness and begin the journey to regain what we once were.

To get to where we can recreate all that we are, we must solve the puzzle of the in-the-way lower order fields, i.e. the electromagnetic controlled overlay of the bio-field and DNA, along with the emotional field and mental field that hold programming to fit us into the base program (aka the ISP). There can be more layers inserted, such as the chakra system, which is regressed Sirian A technology built for the intra-systemic lineages, and other layers we might have created over the span of numerous lifetimes. The lower order fields are inserted to block the higher order energy system from connecting to our organic bio-field and allow our own code systems to unfold, leading us back to the density energies we also are able to process and integrate.

Getting Rid of the Chakra System

The first step is to get rid of the chakra system, if we have activated this in any forms of energy work, along with clearing out everything we created in our fields while working with the chakras. Mantras, symbols, images and frequencies must be cleared out given that they are part of the less functional programs, simulating an activation and ascension paradigm.

Removal of the Chakra System

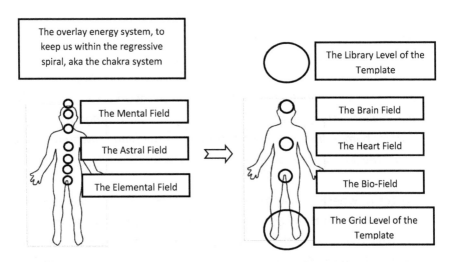

The chakra system holds three layers within each chakra; i.e. the base of each chakra is the elemental layer (etheric), then follows the astral in the middle and finally the mental layer. The chakra system generates, and is part of, the lower order distortion planes.

The Chakras hold Regressed Genetics Too
- The mental layer holds regressed genetics from the reptoid races.
- The astral layer holds regressed genetics from the avian races.
- The etheric layer holds genetics from the regressed insectoid races.
- The organic form holds genetics from the regressed mammal races, which are reengineered to respond to the chakra system.

The regressed genetics in the chakras were activated by the mantras and symbols that were used in the chakra activation work, linking the lower order fields up to the less functional programs. It was made this way, so if a human did get the idea of something higher and wanted to do the uplifting, the chakra system and programs would kick in and lead that human astray into the less functional programs and by that, prevent the true energy system from activating.

Thus, the clearing of what is in the way, also means to let go of what we thought was the way to progress. And it means to understand that we have been tricked into the lesser functional programs. The chakra teaching system is only one of the less functional programs. Any form of teaching system we have used, involving energy work, needs to be looked into and checked if it was part of the programs, allowed by the intra-systemic lineages. The chances are 99%.

Also pay attention to: Although the chakra system, or any other teaching system set up to create energies, has not been activated and worked with in this lifetime, there might be traces of it all in the lower order fields from other lifetimes.

Of course, here some contemplation is needed. Is the HAL Philosophy another one of the less functional programs, claiming to be something and then in fact it is just another deception? There is an old saying: "You know the tree by its fruits." Experience will tell the difference.

Clearing of the Inserted Genetics
Once we have cleared out what we have built ourselves, via the less functional activation programs, we can begin the work with the three lower fields keeping us stuck in the base program, i.e. the Interactive Simulation Program (the ISP) and the I-cubes running this, controlling humanity and creating the world setup we have today.

These layers in the lower order fields contain regressed genetics of a more complex variety and only if we activate them[46] is it possible to clear them out. And that poses a danger, of course, given that we will get in contact with whatever they are tied into, their contributors, the artificial timelines and control technologies. But it has to be done to get rid of our linkup to the regressed 4D-5D and the-there-present organic or holographic humanoids having their balls and chains on us.

Not only are we to do the freeing work, to get out of the harvesting programs under the intra-systemic lineages and their allies, we also have to take the responsibility of clearing out all genetics inserted into us along with shutting down the timelines and technologies they are fueling.[47] We have to do that, given the fact that the inserted genetics in us are upholding the regressed timelines and realities. If we ignore this crucial part of the freeing work, we are accepting the regressed realities to remain connected to our solar system. And then, we are no better than the powers that be.

The inserted regressed genetics are replicated genetics, mostly from insectoid, avian or reptoid humanoid races. Via the inserted genetics running our energy system, the humanoids have access to generate

---

[46] *Terralogy* explains about the inserted regressed genetics and how to activate them. Although shown within the LPU settings the techniques can easily be modified to fit the work now.

[47] Meaning that the work is not just done for us but for the highest good of the many.

what they need of new code systems, develop timelines and generate clones of us or whatever. Or just harvest the genetics, when they are ripe for trade.[48]

All humans hold a variety of replicated genetics from more than one humanoid. The typical number is 3 to 13, but it can be more, all depending on which regressed program, that human is part of. Since the humanoids work on different levels of energy, it is not a problem for them to share the same fields of a human, as they shift in and out when the energies of our reality change during the hours of the day.

The Energetic Parasites
An unfortunate side effect of the inserted regressed genetics is that they generate lots of energetic parasites in our fields. It is so, because the inserted genetics are replicas and impure. Thus, over the course of the month via the joint time share of our organic vessel and energy system, as the regressed races run their merry-go-round of different energies to activate their selection of genetics, we get polluted with dissimilar energetic parasites.

These energetic parasites nest in our mental and emotional fields in the middle of the energy patterns, we have created in this lifetime and previous lifetimes. From their nests in the emotional and mental fields, they can control our choices, what we think is the correct thing to do, all we perceive, all that feels important to us and what we want in life. Including the humans, we attract and events that come our way, which often are the cause-and-effect of the "parasitic calls." The psychological and energetic control, the energetic parasites have on us, is immense.

---

[48] Most of this is happening during night time, when our body is out of function. Then our energy system gets transferred into the 4D facilities. All of this will become clear, once the sight is back. The back tracking – we follow the trail of the inserted genetics - is one of the techniques we need to learn to get rid of our clones there.

When we clear out the energetic parasites, quite a lot of what we thought were important to us vanish with them, along with a scale of irrational and non-constructive emotional responses.[49]

The Human Ego

The ego structure is a biproduct of the dynamics of the three lower fields, i.e. the electromagnetic mental field, the emotional field and the interfered version of the bio-field. The three lower order fields were inserted to rule out our higher order knowledge and awareness capacities that could get activated, when and if, the original energy system, template and consciousness units work appropriately with the organic vessel and bio-field.

Thus, our innate knowledge of how to do timeline and template work, and how to progress using energy and consciousness to do so, are unable to interconnect to and transform the bio-field, because of the lower fields and their blocking of the original bio-field, keeping it focused on the electromagnetic energies.

As long as we play the game of being a base program human - having our energetic processing abilities and our organic vessel occupied with the human world - our entire system quickly adjusts to the energies, we utilize. Upholding the normal human ways and sticking to the base program means to continuously utilize the timeline event energies.

Conversely, the upholding of a progressive higher awareness lifestyle means to completely transform the lower order energies into their

---

[49] How to remove energetic parasites and clearing of our energy patterns, are shown in the Basic Energy Work Class. The removal of the organic-holographic 4th and 5th dimensional entities are in the Advanced Energy Work Class. How to produce higher order energies are in the HAL Advanced Classes 1-2 and the Future Human Project Courses 1-4.

higher order density equivalent. Hence, we cannot sit on both chairs, i.e. being a normal human and doing the progression work, since it is two distinctively different kinds of energy utilization. It is a choice of a lifetime.[50]

The higher order energy systems and the organic vessel with its three lower fields:

Higher Order Energy System – the True Human; Progressive
Consciousness units
Code sheets and template
Energy system fitting the original solar system

Lower Order Fields – the False Human; Regressive
Mind-field to be altered into the brain field
Emotional field to be altered into the heart field
Bio-frequency field to be altered into the bio-density field

Organic form – Molecular
Bio-frequency matter to be cleared by our activation of the higher order energy system, and then returned into density units.

In the transition work we need to be aware of how we utilize energy because the density-matter molecules (as matter molecules in their lower order version and as density units in their higher), composing the organic vessel, do not object to the lack of correct usage.

---

[50] Which is why the HAL Project is focused on the original ways of being human, new ways to work with our food, our surroundings and our body, along with the higher order sciences of how to utilize energy correctly to create. The HAL Project is aimed at giving all the needed information to do the full transition. From what is in the way to what is needed to rebuild. And then, of course, giving ideas to non-profit projects and small businesses, so we can claim a jurisdiction under the progressive networks.

For all that matters, energetically speaking, the organism has a functional bio-field and an ego structure organizing the bio-matter in some sort of imitated evolution. Energy does not discern between a lower order construction or higher order consciousness, since energy is simply energy. Energy is information that unfolds according to the purpose and coding, it has been given.[51]

In essence, our template and energy system are inserted into a reengineered organic vessel with three lower order fields saturated with genetics that are not ours, simulating a present. And yet we are still us, albeit kept occupied in the timelines of the past, where our higher order template, code sheets and energy system have been and are kept busy within the regressed and distorted timelines.

The Above and Below Distortion
The pushing of the progressive and true level of our existence into the semi-artificial holographic worlds of the past, was done to take away any individual momentum of higher order progression capacity along with our true power to work with genetics, consciousness and energy. All in all, *to prevent us from reaching our original functionalities in the now,* if we by any chance got the energies to do so. But this have had dire consequences for the human race.

For far too long, our consciousness genetics have been utilized and harvested in the semi- to completely artificial realities, by making our template produce genetics serviceable for the regressed worlds. In that procedure, replicas of our higher order templates have been dried out until evaporation in the completely artificial worlds, or left behind as depleted shells, holding our genetics on various timelines in the semi-artificial holographic realities. But it does not end there. Aside from the depleted shells with their dried-out genetics, the semi-

---

[51] Hence, to get back on track, we must use the Laws and the Principles to ensure the correct usage of energy. All the human ways are programmed to create distortion.

artificial holographic realities and their timelines are equally inhabited by hollowed-out template and energy system clones and duplicates.[52]

These unwilling and non-consented additional versions of us – the many clones, replicates and duplicates - are the production leftovers from reengineered organic to holographic representations of us, all made with the purpose of keeping the artificial worlds and timelines operational.

Plus, not to forget, as the regressed races are done with whatever they came here to do and move into other parallel systems to work, they just leave behind their miscellanies and trash, including their left-behind technologies and dysfunctional androids. Altogether and in total, generating the upper distortion fields. *The upper dimensional distortion fields* surround our reality in concentric circles and they are the final result of a rude and no-caring utilization of reality energies, humanity and all lifeforms here. They also play a role in preventing us from accessing the higher progressive worlds.

It might appear as the spiral of bad news just goes on and on. And in a way it does. 12500 years of downsizing has had its toll on our energy system. We have lived too many lives participating in the regressed worlds. And we have to work our way back through all of our layers to free ourselves from their timelines. The climate and environmental issues[53] are a reflection of the state our entire reality is in.

The upside is that we grow with the clearing work and become better at it, as we move through the timelines and what we learn from doing the work. From our endeavors, we get to remember who we are and the power we truly hold. Fear will wear out; strength will come back in.

---

[52] Quite similar to our present-day world.
[53] And, not to forget, space junk will also become a big problem in the future.

On top of this, *the lower dimensional distortion fields* are affecting us on a totally unconscious level connected to our original bio-field. This deliberate pollution of the racial networks originates from exhausted holographic replicates, duplicates and semi-holographic to completely organic clones that exist in the lower dimensions of our reality, living in absolute agony and despair above and below the earth's crust.[54] These creatures always look for sources to feed from and give them energy.

Consequently, the adjacent semi-artificial holographic realities above and below, and their remnant timelines are full of depleted shells and hollowed-out entities. These layers of energetic distortion above and below our present-day world, compose horrifying energetic to semi-organic realities beyond human imagination. It is so, because these barely human remnants carry the memory imprints of what they have been used for, and the timelines they have been used on.

All cultural myths and religions speak of such realities. These realities are not a figment of imagination created by the primitive cultures, as science believes today. But it takes one to know, before accepting it and then, naturally, getting it lifted out of its religious, or older human interpretations, and into the correct higher order perspectives so we can transform what we encounter in the appropriate ways.

But the unfortunate use of genetics and energy does not end with the upper and lower dimensional distortion fields, done by the regressed

---

[54] The distorted holographic realities, below the earth's crust, are often referred to as the underworld. These realities - there are 7 layers - have been generated over long periods of time, and as the earth changed and pushed the old continents below the surface, the human remnants of these worlds become part of the underworld aka the fall zones. The fall zones are positioned in the 1-2 dimensions and they distort the racial network with the left-behind depleted and contaminated genetics.

races. Our humanity plays an equally large role in polluting their own environment on a daily basis. Not just on the outside in the forms of wrongful use of energy and natural resources.

Inside our world, on the energetic levels, humans are creating *the collective human distortion planes.* These are comprised of decades of emotional reactions and thought forms generated by the lower order fields and their energetic parasites, as well as the left-behind ghosts and lost "souls." Ghosts and lost souls are the remaining shells of the lower order bio-, emotional and mental fields, stuck on *the collective human distortion planes* kept alive by the inserted regressed genetics.

Hence, we have *the upper and lower distortion fields* affecting the resonance fields composed of holographic-regressed garbage, due to wrongful use of density energies and depleted consciousness units, and we have *the human collective distortion planes* fully intertwined with the human psyche and mind, originating from the wrongful use of the bio-field, the emotional and mental fields, and their inserted fragmented regressed genetics.

Goals to Set
The first goal is to clear what we hold of distorted energies from *the collective human distortion planes*. This is done by transforming the lower fields to be able to hold the density energies similar to the ones found in our higher order energy system. That is the first important clearing work and something all humans should do. Sometime in the future, humanity will learn to think and feel in proper, non-polluting ways. The three lower fields should become permeable and harmless.

Then later on, as we know more, we can begin the work to undo the big divide between the higher and lower fields in us by clearing out *the upper and lower distortion fields* connected to us. Within this work, we recreate ourselves as a unified composition of energy and consciousness, integrated into the organic vessel, we have today.

The Step by Step Transition

What the individual human can do, begins with the ongoing process of transition. We do that by making the needed changes in our life to accommodate for space to do the inner work.

When the outer settings of our human lives are arranged in ways, where we can do the transition processes, we begin the daily energy and clearing work to pave the way for a reconnection to the template and original energy system.

The transformation of the emotional and mental fields is part of the initial clearing work to enable us to reconnect to the higher order energy system, because the emotional and mental fields are blocking our inner perception, sensing and understanding of the true worlds.

The next step of the energy work is centered around the removal of the psychological effects on our ego structure from the regressed genetic fragments. These inserted regressed fragments are not ours, and they are loaded with false memories and connected to timelines, within artificial holographic realities, or connected to the regressed 4D-5D worlds, which used to be part of the progressive worlds in our solar system, albeit altered to fit the regressed races.

When the transition work with the ego, the emotional and mental fields are moving well along, and we have learned to some degree to work with our higher order energy system, we can begin the work of adapting the organic vessel and its bio-field to match the incoming progressive energies of the NGC.

And here, just to point it out again; it is the consciousness units, the code sheets and the true energy system that are important, when we talk about preserving the 12 universal human lineages – it is never the organic vessels, contrary to what many believe today. The organic forms vary from age to age and thus the organic version of a human is not significant, in the discussion of what is important to preserve for future generations.

Consequently, it is the consciousness units running the template, the advanced engineered code sheets and the energy systems, which are important in the long run. These are to be the main focus in our work. Besides, the humans of the future will get a different organic form.

Mastery of a Daily Routine

Even though the organic vessel is subsidiary and merely a tool to exist within realities, we take good care of our organic form to achieve the best circumstances for our existence.

We keep it fit and in as high an energetic state as possible. Food plays a huge role in this and therefore we choose the best herbivore or frugivore nutrition, giving it the conditions from which the organic vessel can function perfectly. We prioritize this task to enable us to do our progression work without any physical block-stoppers.

Mastering reality and energy is not just a mental exercise done in meditation, it is the daily routine of doing the transition and clearing work by developing ourselves emotionally and mentally in challenges, we freely take onto ourselves, along with making our own food by using the best vegetables, fruits, nuts and seeds, and by planning and preparing it ourselves.

Daily Exercise

Daily exercise is required to build solid bone- and muscle structures, in becoming agile and alert, along with the extra oxygenation of the blood, leading to a better metabolism and well-being.[55]

The heart's muscle must be strengthened through various forms of cardio exercises, appropriate to our organic composition. A strong heart is needed, when the higher order energies begin to bridge into our organic vessel. The bridging begins with the heart field, and if the

---

[55] https://en.wikipedia.org/wiki/Oxygen_saturation_(medicine)

heart is weak, it will not respond well to the higher order energies. It should also be noted that the organic vessel undergoes fluctuations, having day to day variations and different energetic compositions, as we progress and lift in energy – aside from the regressed merry-go-round. It changes, because we make changes to our energy system.

And, naturally, allowing for days with rest and contemplation. On these days, we decide where we want to go, what challenges we are to set for ourselves and we create the strategies to get there, as well as the setting the goals of our clearing work.

From the lot of our inner and outer work, and by implementing the Principles, Laws and Rules into our lives as the guiding techniques in the choices, we are to make to reach the highest purity rate, the highest standards and the highest progression rate, we learn how to rebuild the density energy system. And in our inner work with that, we learn how to implement the higher order knowledge and access the progressive sciences, we also hold.

If Only......

The first steps towards a possible future, where we could play a part in the full transitioning of our reality into a higher order reality, begin with us taking responsibility for our own health and constitution by becoming herbivores or frugivores. The honoring of life, utilizing the lifeforce in its correct ways, along with the respect for other lifeforms begin with that choice and the changes of our lifestyle, it takes.

It also entails the inner work of transforming our emotional field by working our way through our suppressed emotional patterns and dealing with our subconscious material. From the learning processes with transforming the psyche, it is easy to adapt the methodology of the psychological work into the higher order clearing and inner work, where we erase and alter timelines. In other words; the method we utilized to clear and evaporate the energy patterns in our emotional field, we similarly use in the timeline work.

Along with this work, we also have to have a self-driven need to seek new information and preferably take higher educations, learning how to learn, and instigate self-studies using the free materials from various universities on the Internet. The goal is to build a processing, discerning and knowledgeable brain structure.

From that basis, it is easy to bridge to the higher order sciences, if – of course – we can move beyond the scientific paradigms and into the pioneering paradigms, to invent new ways of perceiving reality.

We do this with the goals of becoming able to engineer new skills, create lead innovations, come up with inventive sciences and original ways of being human. We aim for an advanced global humanity, living in harmony with our reality and all lifeforms in non-exploiting ways.

The more we work with the NGC energies, activate and cleanup, the more of our original genetics we will have at our disposal as the NGC hits the collective racial level of the 2-8 pillar in 2026, and the easier it will be for us to meetup with the challenges the next stage is going to pose.

In the NGC transition period between 2017-2025, we are to work with the reality field energies. This means the overall field we are part of

1. *The resonance fields.*
2. *The grids (the holographic energy circulation of our reality).*
3. *The racial network, used when we were seeded in a long time ago. It corresponds with the template and fuels the level of the pillar we had reached before the timeline event.*

Which takes us to the really difficult part of our clearing work.

The Reality Jurisdictions

Our reality is surrounded by concentric circles of distorted energy. And then we have our outer world as well. From the earlier HAL material:

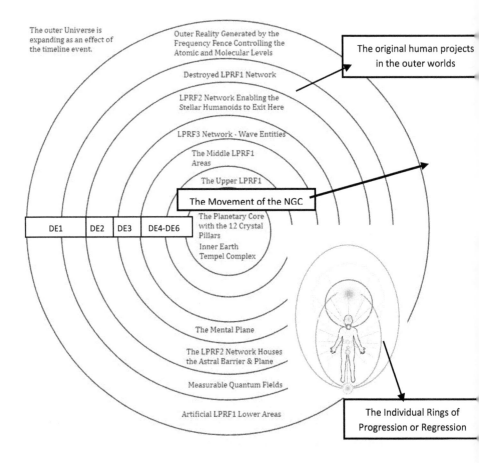

The outer Universe is expanding as an effect of the timeline event.

Outer Reality Generated by the Frequency Fence Controlling the Atomic and Molecular Levels

Destroyed LPRF1 Network

LPRF2 Network Enabling the Stellar Humanoids to Exit Here

LPRF3 Network - Wave Entities

The Middle LPRF1 Areas

The Upper LPRF1

The Movement of the NGC

The Planetary Core with the 12 Crystal Pillars

Inner Earth Tempel Complex

The Mental Plane

The LPRF2 Network Houses the Astral Barrier & Plane

Measurable Quantum Fields

Artificial LPRF1 Lower Areas

DE1	DE2	DE3	DE4-DE6

The original human projects in the outer worlds

The Individual Rings of Progression or Regression

We are to work our way pass the other-dimensional regressed zones.

To meet up with the NGC transition challenges, hitting our reality in the years to come, important understandings must be addressed to fully grasp the implications of the energy work needed to match the energies of the NGC as they unfold into the racial activation cycle on a collective level, to activate and cleanup the failed genetics within the human projects as a whole, and followed by the individual activation cycle, where the ancient pillar project genetics will be activated for a cleanup or continuation.[56] The NGC transition work, in a more straight forward version, has been addressed. In the upcoming chapters, the clearing work on the more challenging levels will be addressed.

This information is given now, so that the ones that are ready to begin as the first of many, can be up front with the transition work before it hits on a global scale. Because, as the NGC hits the human population, the wave of changes and challenges cannot be predicted due to a high possibility rate of unknowns. The unknowns are the inserted regressed genetics and how these will respond to the NGC, as well as how the general population will respond to the incoming higher energies.

We must work for the best possible futures, by foreseeing what they hold of potentials and alter these while we can in the present. That is part of the heart field clearing and rebuilding work.

At the same time, we must transform what has become the now and turn whatever has been manifested into its highest potentials as part of the clearing and rebuilding of the brain field and bio-field. We do this work to remove any momentum of a possible future, where we are positioned in the cold dying DE1 universe. And if necessary, we must go into previous cycles and timelines to find the root of the existing manifestations and clear these out entirely.

---

[56] In this phase, if there are no present-day humans able to implement the template and its genetics into their organic vessel, the genetics will be retracted to the Library.

Although the ISP and its many I-cubes will cease to function correctly, following the incoming energies of the NGC, the inserted genetics will remain active in all humans, because they are uninterruptedly fueled from the 4th dimension and technologies positioned outside our world. These technologies will ensure that whatever is cleared by the NGC, will be replaced for as long as possible.[57]

Which leads us to the really difficult part, because the regressed races will keep their jurisdictions, as one of the 5 reality zones, along with their inserted control programs, scan and patch-up technologies. The prohibiting technologies will continue to work on an individual level, because of the relative reality dynamics.

Thus, a relative reality is not necessary an outer location. It can be an inner as well. The reality dynamics work equally in progressive and regressive systems, since all realities in our universe were once part of the progressive systems. *So, what are the deeper consequences and implications of this?*

The Reality Zones and Inner Jurisdiction
A human is an individual energy field within a collective energy field. The state of the fields in a human defines which part of the regressed or progressed realities, it is part of due to *the Laws of energetic and*

---

[57] The constant relooping of timelines is done by the intra-systemic lineages that want to uphold the regressed programs controlling our reality. The more frequently they reloop the regressed timelines, the more depleted the grids get. Each reloop of a group of timelines always demands a high amount of energy, and it has to be taken from somewhere. The numerous hadron colliders and particle accelerators around the globe are part of the quantum field stimulation to enable the relooping to manifest into the lower outer grids. Humans are in their many scientific experiments helping the regressed races to control, deplete and harm our reality. The climate changes are one of the results of the over-excessive use of quantum energy and not just an issue due to fossil fuels, pollution and overpopulation.
https://en.wikipedia.org/wiki/List_of_accelerators_in_particle_physics

genetic affinity. Hence, what a human hold of energetic distortion, regressed genetics and prohibiting technologies will determine how long that human remains unaware and non-activated. It is so because of the emplacement into the 5 reality zones, although huge portions of the regressed programs and technologies underwent an activation and cleanup in the systemic activation cycle. But not everything, and thus the manifestation of the regressed reality zone.

Subsequently, the humans that live in the regressed reality zone under the jurisdiction of the intra-systemic lineages, lunar human races etc., will not sense the effect of the incoming energies of the NGC due to constant relooping, manipulation and overriding of the NGC energies, done by the regressed races controlling these inner and outer areas.

The regressed reality zone remains as part of our system because of the anti-progressive intra-systemic humans and the here-living lunar human races, along with their regressed human hybrids, from both of these factions, living inside our reality.[58] *They are strengthening the possibility of a regressed reality zone.*

Similarly, if we can activate our progressive consciousness and energy system, and implement this into our present-day human vessel, we can manifest the possibility of the 6-12 human reality zone, also part of the 5 reality zones.

Unfortunately, we cannot touch the areas under the jurisdiction of the regressed races, the intra-systemic humans and the lunar human

---

[58] A regressed human hybrid is living inside our reality. They are engineered into that version of a human, the regressed need to keep our reality status quo. He or she typically does not know what they are, but their mindset is archaic and always in the range of creating negativity and standing tall in any anti-progressive direction.

races, since we have no claims over their inserted racial grids. This is only possible, if they hand over and leave. Then we can clear out their grids etc.

With this statement it is to be acknowledged that the racial grids consist of numerous transferred minor grids from the regressed and infected other realities in our vicinity, as well as from the planets in our solar system. To name a few, e.g. Egypt is technically built upon the left-over viable racial grid from Mars, although fully altered by the Orions, and northern Europe is built upon sections of the racial grid that was used in the last Atlantis. It is so, because the last pieces of the Atlantean grid were first transferred to northern Africa, to allow for the last seeding of the original human projects, and later on it was removed into northern Europe, as part of the 12 Sisters network. The last transfer happened, when Africa fell into the hands of the Orions due to the trade-off done by the regressed Sirian As.

It is important to understand that there are no earth humans as in the normal conceptualization. The base program keeps up the deception that there is an earth humanity. In fact, all humans are semi to fully regressed aliens – to use that word.

Some humans are deliberately covering up what they truly are by the means of advanced overlay and holographic deception technologies. These are mainly the intra-systemic lineages in control of the base program, although they prefer to live in adjacent realities and only have a counterpart in this world, when needed.

Or they are here as other-reality human and humanoid races having been transferred to our system, as their own reality fell, similar to the story of the lunar races.

134

Technically, we are all alien to this reality, since none of us are part of the original Er'Th grids. The only true humans are the 6-12 humans and they took off a long time ago to protect the highest purity rate, the highest standards and the highest progression rate in the original human racial grid and thus the complete universal program. The 6-12 humanity will return after the completion of the NGC and activate the original racial grid.

In the meantime, we are to try to regain our capacities, as the races we truly are, and get as close as we can to the original human version, we had in the Workstations and within the pillar programs, we were part of before the timeline event. From that stance of knowledge, we will know if we want to stay – after the NGC is completed – or return to our own systems, which have been reset too.

Hence, we must remember in the strife to regain what we are, we are not fighting invading aliens, but infected and regressed human races stemming from the original 12 human lineages.[59]

Part of the awakening process is to claim the full connection to our original racial grid and then how we want to live, as well as regaining the position as equals within the racial density worlds. As the higher order dimensions bleed through into our reality, it will be easier for us to work for this, because we can see what we are up against.

---

[59] Even the SSN future humans will come to that conclusion at some point, and then alter their programs here. They will hopefully change their human projects to a new line of racial engineering, to accommodate for the NGC. The human-humanoid covert military projects will reach that conclusion, probably sometime in 2020, as humanity gets emplaced into their correct racial grid. If the humans taking part in the covert military programs accept this, their stand on maintaining their faulty hybrid projects will fall, because their premise is that we are up against an alien invasion. If they acknowledge they are the aliens, their programs will be shut down, and that would be a big win for us all. The probability rate for that to happen is 60%.

Choosing Where to Live

The question of which outer area to live in, cannot be based upon "a feeling good" about the area or if the sun is shining, but upon what is going on in the other dimensions behind that area, and which race that has the jurisdiction of it. It is up to us to find an area, where we as a minimum can do the transition work, without having harvested what we produce, and are allowed to generate our jurisdiction, cf. the 5 reality zones. Which, for now is a lot to ask.

For now, certain areas are worse than others to reside in, but de facto there are no safe areas, since our reality and its surface areas have been controlled by the regressed races for at least 12500 years, and they are very territorial. The world we live in is a checkerboard reality, and it is up to us to find the places where we can work and do what we have to do to ensure our own space.

So, what could be considered better areas to live in are the areas where the remaining regressed races are trying to change their ways and follow the energies of the NGC. These areas will transition into the progressive settings, although extremely slowly and we will have to endure their unhurried process and whatever follows with that, i.e. their own transition difficulties, their internal fights and inter-racial disputes, along with their attempts to cut their losses.

Another alternative is an area that have been abandoned by the regressed races. Unfortunately, this means the racial grids have been depleted and most likely the area is connected to the 1-2D.[60]

A depletion of the racial grid is the only reason why a regressed race leaves a territory. Depleted areas with too low energy, make it difficult for us to do our clearing work, since we technically live in a dead-zone and thereby directly on top of a fall zone. The lower fields and our organic vessel will adjust to the extremely low energies, and

---

[60] As everything else leaves, the fall zone 1D entities and semi-organic 2D faulty races of the extremely old worlds take over the control of the area.

before we know of it, we are part of a horror movie, because as we drop in energy, whatever is beneath us can get access.[61]

Thus, choosing to live in a depleted area would be like living in a poisonous swamp full of unwarranted lifeforms, or in a desert with no oxygen and water, with daily gushes of hot unbreathable air. That is similar to what happened on Mars and why the there-living human races, insectoid and avian races transferred to our planet.[62]

Another possible scenario could be joint areas where treaties are arranged, and we live side by side. In all possibilities, we have to work with the understanding that the regressed races can return to claim their grids, once we have made the grids and areas viable through our transformative energy work, or they shift side overnight as they have done throughout history and if so selling us out, because we live in their jurisdiction, to whomever have made new alliances with them. They cannot be trusted at all. History has taught us that.

The 4th dimension inhabited by regressed androids, insectoid, avian, reptoid and lower leveled mammal humanoids. Unfortunately, it is the first level of density perception, we encounter, when we have cleared what keep us connected to the collective human distortion planes. It cannot be avoided, because the inserted regressed genetics typically stem from these 4th dimensional regressed races.[63]

---

[61] Genetic and energetic affinity have many different possibilities and outcomes.

[62] At some point the human diseases, caused by other-reality bacteria, will come to our attention. The old microbes will come to life because of the NGC, creating new mysterious viruses. E.g. some of the bacteria, which got to our world from Mars in the grid transfer, are not indigenous to our reality.

The solar system map of our bio-regenesis defines which bacteria we are immune to.

[63] The humanoids have freely given their genetics to the intra-systemic lineages as part of an agreement, where the 4Ds got jurisdictions and trade routes in our system in turn for their genetics. The intra-systemics have used these genetics as an attempt to heal their own regressed human genetics, from the standpoint of mending their older forms of genetics by the use of the humanoid genetics. This has failed.

It is important to acknowledge that all regressed races are notorious liars and utterly service to self. They have become humanoids with a predatorial mindset. They have lost all higher order standings. On top of that, they use advanced technologies along with holographic 4-5D drones and androids to uphold and maintain their jurisdictions and their human projects in the surface areas.

We must see through all of their deception and cloaking technologies, making them appear human in any forms of encounter. We cannot let us be deceived in this completion cycle and repeat the same mistakes of the past.

It is time to prove that we have learned from the past, and are making the right choices of freedom.

As the energies change exponentially, throughout the activation and cleanup phases of the NGC, the other dimensions will permeate into our reality and we will learn the direct way, if we are welcome or not in our home and in the city, we have chosen to live in.

The level of direct interference, harvesting and terror will become evident, if we are not welcome in a territorial dispute. If we cannot handle what is allowing the other-dimensional races to operate in our area, or find a suitable solution by e.g. claiming jurisdiction and do what it takes to win over a space, we can live in, the best option is to leave. If we leave, the territorial issues will not go away, since the next area we might move into, holds other or similar issues.

However, we can find areas that provide for space, where we can do the work – we might have to move a lot - but whenever we do, it must always be under great caution until we are through the various timelines of the regressed races, and we have cleared out all genetics making us partake in their jurisdictions.

All regressed dimensions hold a number of artificial or semi-organic worlds and many timelines. And they are connected to our reality.

Adjacent Reality Perception and Timeline Clearing Work in Density 1 – D1-3

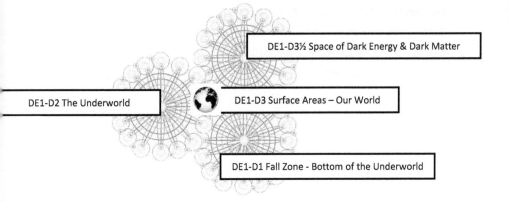

DE1-D3½ Space of Dark Energy & Dark Matter

DE1-D2 The Underworld

DE1-D3 Surface Areas – Our World

DE1-D1 Fall Zone - Bottom of the Underworld

Adjacent Reality Perception and Timeline Clearing Work in Density 2 – D4-6

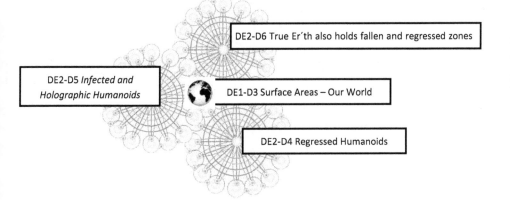

DE2-D6 True Er'th also holds fallen and regressed zones

DE2-D5 *Infected and Holographic Humanoids*

DE1-D3 Surface Areas – Our World

DE2-D4 Regressed Humanoids

As we transit through the various phases of energy work, our inner perception of the dimensional worlds will change accordingly. What we see all depends on which density level we are working on.

Our energy system and genetics determine the other-dimensional worlds and the timelines we can clear and interact with.

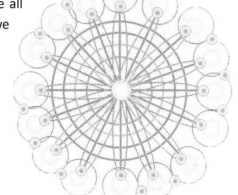

The regressed worlds, including ours, are all built up as a cross

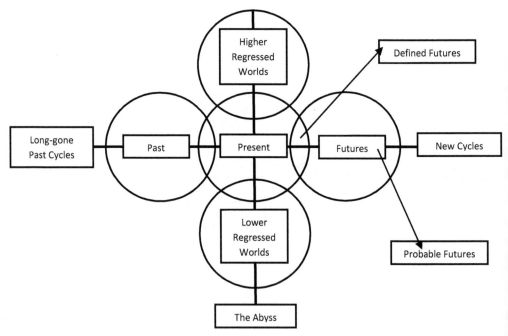

The distorted dimensional energy body

The regressed density fields are to be cleared of regressed genetics.

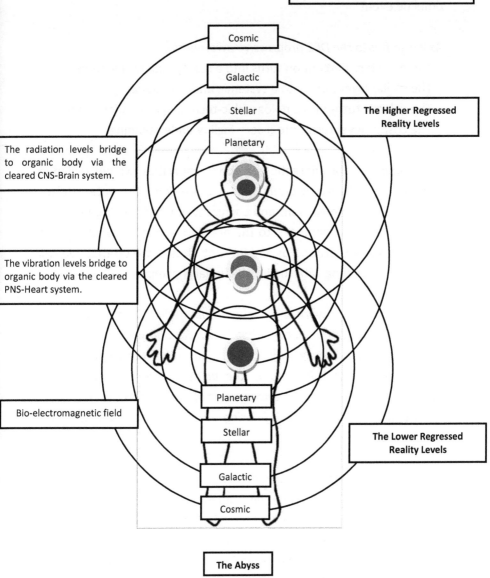

Cosmic

Galactic

Stellar

The Higher Regressed Reality Levels

Planetary

The radiation levels bridge to organic body via the cleared CNS-Brain system.

The vibration levels bridge to organic body via the cleared PNS-Heart system.

Bio-electromagnetic field

Planetary

Stellar

The Lower Regressed Reality Levels

Galactic

Cosmic

The Abyss

Shift of Perspective
The planetary, stellar, galactic and cosmic levels are how they appear to us within the DE1 matter reality. These levels are remnants of the timeline event.

As we shift into the DE2 progressive awareness
- The planetary perception turns into a reality field understanding.
- The stellar level turns into a systemic understanding.
- The galactic turns into a holographic-technological understanding.
- The cosmic level turns into a core facility understanding.

As we upgrade our energetic perception capacities, we get skilled in exercising *the double awareness,* i.e. we are doing the outer surface thing while being observant and cognizant of what is going on in the other dimensions connected to the area, we are in, or what is going on in the humans around us and in front of us. If we do that, we will get better at dealing with the jurisdictional challenges.

The NGC transition work is not about doing what is easy and within our comfort zone, but about what is correct and honorable. Taking short-cuts and the easy way is the signature of the regressed and humanoid mindset. It is up to us to educate and develop ourselves to be able to process these advanced levels of reality, acknowledge what we are in the middle of, and figuring out how to deal with what we encounter.

The End of the Regressed Occupation
Without the NGC, the regressed humanoid occupation of the other dimensions would continue until they decided to leave, or the original human racial grids get so depleted that the regressed races cannot be bothered staying there. The depletion would be the consequence of

their constant relooping. Whenever the regressed races reloop their jurisdictions into a new or secondary timeline branch, the original human racial grids and their humanoid racial grids get depleted. They reloop to keep the completion cycle of the timeline event at bay.[64]

Whenever a timeline event branch dries out, the regressed races reloop their merry-go-round into a similar branch, to continue their affairs in the new branch after having transferred everything into the new branch.

If an overall depletion should happen, all the racial grids of our system would reset to the original settings of the Ancient Ones, excluding all humanoids from returning. It would eventually take out humanity too.

Nonetheless, the NGC is going to play a huge role by changing the trajectory of events. For now, the regressed races think they have the completion cycle under control, but the facts are something entirely else.[65]

In 2017-2019 the NGC worked its way through the 3rd cycle grids within our reality and then within the higher order resonance fields, clearing out the ancient timelines in the proximity of the original blast of the timeline event. This was done to release the perimeter of the timeline event from the resonance fields, allowing the echo of the timeline event to leave our system and continue into the past version of the 3rd cycle, reversing the event and pulling most of the 3rd cycle energies back to where they belonged. A lot of very old stuff left with that, and thus the effects were not huge in our world, seen from a

---

[64] The completion cycle is ending the foundation of the worlds that arose as a result of the timeline event, pushing all timelines back to their original trajectory. The intra-systemics and the regressed are trying to find solutions to continue their existence, which is the reason for the constant relooping.

[65] It should be noted that most of the regressed races and the intra-systemics think the NGC is a strategic hoax from the progressives to get their territories back.

regressed race perspective, aside from the effects on the racial grids within our world, running on the 3rd cycle energies. We have seen the effects of this in the ancient worlds, i.e. beneath equator.[66]

For the intra-systemics and the regressed races this result could just as easily have been a side effect of the TE completion cycle. But beneath the retraction of the timeline event await the humongous energetic waves of the NGC. Given the fact, that until 1999 the NGC was only working within the other progressive systems and between 2000-2016, it was working on the old progressive areas in our system, the regressed have not noticed it, but this will change.

From 2020-2022 the NGC runs through the middle sections of our system, reaching the DE2 to be accompanied by the shift of the sun in 2022, where the sun goes into its progressive DE2 version, shedding off its DE1 timeline event version. The shift of the sun will amplify the progressive energies in all resonance fields and holographic grids on a D4-D6 level, which the regressed races have calculated with, given that most of their trade stations, planetoid facilities etc. are situated in the 4-5D of our system.[67]

But, as the sun shifts into its original energetic composition, it will regain its position and from that stance it will get a huge boost from the incoming energies of the NGC. The regressed have not measured in that boost of energy into their plans, nor have they calculated with the re-amplification between the NGC energies and the energies of the original sun, and the implications of this.

---

[66] The effects seem huge for humans because of their restrictions. If humans had had their intrinsic knowledge of how to work with energy, then the extreme weather, the wildfires and odd old viruses would not have surfaced as they did. The effects of the NGC could have been alleviated long before these events reached the state, where they had to go into manifestation. Once that point is reached, the manifestation cycle has to run its course.

[67] Due to the completion of the timeline event, the repositioning of the sun was expected along with similar events, correcting the effects of the timeline event.

As the NGC hits the regressed DE2 dimensions attached to our reality, the regressed humanoid genetics will activate, because they initially were engineered to partake in the original pillar project.[68]

This is so, despite of the genetic alterations in the timeline event, given that the foundational genetic code system stem from the pillar project. Following this, the humanoid genetics will attempt to match the incoming energies, which amplify for activation and growth in all pillar project genetics.

But since the regressed genetics were modified to repel the infection back in the old days, the humanoid genetics will mutate instead, as the energies of the NGC push them into activation and cleanup. This will have unforeseen consequences and most likely the effects of this will not be for the good. This goes for the inserted regressed genetics in humans as well.

The viable humanoid genetics will be reset to their progressive pillar version and then work against the humanoid code systems. The non-viable humanoid genetics will activate and then go into evaporation, and quite quickly. Technically, the regressed races will have to follow the resetting or leave, if they want to remain what they are.[69]

Then, in 2023-2025 the NGC will hit the major holographic grids and the DE2 and DE1 racial grids, preparing for the collective 2-8 pillar activation and cleanup in 2026 and onward. Once the NGC hits our reality in 2026, the intra-systemics and the lunar human races will be hit by the incoming energies of the NGC along with humanity, which will be affected by the genetic activation, cleanup and breakdown.

---

[68] Which none of the regressed or the intra-systemics have taken into consideration.
[69] The modification of the humanoid genetics was only possible due to the timeline event energies, which of course have been part of their many genetic experiments to figure out how to solve that equation. Essentially, they are a dying race.

The emplacement into the 5 reality zones have implications as well, because as long as the regressed races, the intra-systemics and the lunar human races do not believe in the NGC, they will go on with business as usual – that means working on solutions to continue their existence. And unfortunately, humanity is key to that project.

The attempts to crack the code of the genetic regenesis by the use of the templates connected to unaware humans, will still be in play until the regressed races, the intra-systemics and the lunars get that they are in trouble beyond their reach. Not only because the timeline event is ending but because the NGC is for real.

Until they get this, we will struggle with the old racial contracts and the prohibiting technologies due to the relative reality dynamics. Thus, we cannot sit and do nothing, waiting for the NGC to solve our issues.

As mentioned above, the NGC will activate regressed and humanoid genetics, but only the viable ones and they will mutate because of the inserted humanoid code systems. And all humans hold a lot of non-viable regressed genetics. This is why the cleanup and transition work are so important for us to do.

Transition Alleviation
Transforming areas to assist with the unfolding of the energies of the NGC into the surface areas, to make the transition easier, would be a possibility. However, the NGC alleviation work is not about a group of humans meeting up in a circle and sending heart energy to the racial grids. This type of work distorts the grids further.

Although, a lot of work – in the near future – needs to be done by activated progressive humans, residing in areas with progressive grids to alleviate the transition process, but again, only by the ones that are in-the-know of the 3-9 reality grid sciences and completely know how to work holographically with the pillar 5-11 holographic-technologies behind the original progressive developmental programs. The original program cubes are still in place in these areas but in a higher density and shut down for now, as they have been taken over or replaced by the regressed cubes. Along with the knowledge of how to work with these technologies and programs and how they interconnect with the racial and holographic grids.

The accurate reality grid work is about
-   Recoding the holographic grids.
-   Removal of regressed programs and bugs.
-   Reprogramming the code sequences in the core technologies.
-   Taking the areas off the hands of the regressed races and the intra-systemics by clearing the racial grids.
-   And after having got the overall areas, their racial grids and original outpost laboratories back into our custody, then how to work with the NGC energies to reset all into the settings of the 6-12 progressive races.

The Old Racial Contracts

The Background

In the final phases of the take-over of our universe, only a few chose to fight the suppressors. Not many of the progressive humans chose to partake in the end-battles and thus, the few that did, lost the fight to the taking-over races. After the intra-systemic lineages had sold us out, naturally. The last warriors suffered the strongest retaliation and incarceration. They got their templates chopped up and sold off, their genetics harvested and put into plasma vials to be used for trade, and their original organic vessels were put in stasis arrangements by the buyers for further cloning and DNA replication.[70]

The non-fighting pillar humans made survival arrangements with their suppressors, not knowing the consequences of their choices and apparently, having forgotten the accord of the first of the many.[71]

To their defense, they did so under the recommendation of the not-having-shown-their-true-colors-yet intra-systemic lineages and a small group of infiltrated Elders.

The suppressors offered certain conditions and since most of the remaining pillar humans had seen what happened to the ones who declined the conditions – and they technically had no home to return to - the majority consented to the regressed terms.

In this, the remaining humans thought it would prolong their lives and that intervention eventually had to come from the progressive worlds with solutions to change the agreements. It was thought so, since the arrangements were based upon unlawful use of the racial

---

[70] I am ridding the stasis facilities and releasing the genetics of the humans long gone.
[71] It would have been more honorable to fight and lose, than the selling out.

grids and by overtaking, using brute force. A violation of all laws and rules. Nonetheless, help never came due to the manipulation of the higher order councils and what transpired there.[72]

The survival arrangements, agreed to by the remaining humans, were presented to the councils as a deliberate and free choice done by the non-infected humans. It was presented to the councils, as if the pillar humans wanted to continue their evolutionary cycles as part of the humanoid worlds. Naturally, the regressed races used the progressive laws and dynamics in this and thus the higher order councils could not intervene.

The reengineering began, producing the humans into the version we have today. Along with the Elders, that arranged the deals with the regressed races, all the humans that consented to the arrangements stepped into the "new world" under the siege of the regressed races.

To this day all the descendants and lineages stemming from this group of humans – originating on this and the other realities in our system - are bound by the survival arrangements. And that means the majority of humanity.

Today the survival arrangements have been turned into contracts of enslavement and exploitation, for the reason that they have been sold off many times to other regressed races from parallel systems, not caring where the contracts originally came from.

Ending the Contracts
Getting out of the contracts and the exploitation arrangements made by our ancestors is a piece of work every man and woman must do on

---

[72] The hope of intervention is deeply embedded into the human subconscious that one day help will come. Religion plays on the concept of divine intervention and the making of a better world, when the true ones from the heavens return.

their own. It is the wide-ranging stand-up-against the regressed races and claim the rights to become a freed person, and then face up to what is required to get released from the ancient contracts.[73]

While we are in that process, we must also do the clearing work of the regressed genetics,[74] showing that we do not want them in our energy system. We additionally need to clear the regressed genetics so we, energetically, can change our relative reality position and get out of any regressed jurisdictions, since the contracts are part of this.

The higher order councils still cannot intervene into the deals made by the old lineages. Not until the descendants of the remaining humans are able to get rid of their own contracts, will they be set free. And not until the descendants of the Elders, that advocated for the survival arrangements, holographically call in the councils and arrange for an assembly where they annul and nullify the original arrangements, can humanity be set free as a whole.[75]

The Freeing Work

The freeing work begins by holographically calling in the suppressors in an act of emancipation. However, this is not a simple thing to do. If a human utters the statements[76] from within the level of the normal human mind, it does not work. It only works in a self-created direct holographic confrontation with the contract owner, to demand to be

---

[73] A contract is a specific coding of the energy system along with symbol insertions and technologies to uphold the programming. It is not a piece of paper that can be torn apart.

[74] The book *Terralogy* shows how to activate the regressed genetics and then in the HAL Basic and Advanced Energy Work Classes examples are shown of how to deal with what surfaces from the activation work.

[75] I have tried, using my seniority. But since I did not make the initial agreements, I cannot annul them either. What is created can only be undone by its creators. There is no such thing as a stand-in savior.

[76] In the HAL material I give an idea of what such statements would sound like.

150

released. This means expanded awareness and know-how to be able to function on and create access to the other-dimensional realities.

In such an act of emancipation, we claim our rights, demand our genetics released of all exploitation and a giving back of the rights of our racial heritage, as an equal by having become one in our clearing work of the regressed genetics. And, we take the stand of segregating ourselves from the intra-systemic human lineages that sold out their true ancestry in dishonor. And then the game is on.

Furthermore, any contract and its implications depend on which faction of the regressed races, it was made with and how to end its responsibilities will follow from what that race expects. To get this, a direct confrontation where the contract is shown in full, is needed.

In the freeing work, which can take months, we have to decline any favors, inserted regressed genetics and the subsequent powers, these contracts have granted us inside the base program. Whatever the old contracts have given us in insignificant portions inside this world, the regressed have harvested in tenfold in their worlds.

We need to be fully free of all regressed dynamics and arrangements, and then return energetically to the progressive grids, where our work will be rewarded according to the progression spiral dynamics.

Being under contract does not mean to be poor or without powers. On the contrary. Some of the most powerful healers over time have been under contract and operated inside this reality on the behalf of the regressed races. Strong influencers too, and scientists etc.[77]

---

[77] The regressed enjoy taking a pillar human template, insert it into re-engineered human vessels within the base program. Here the humans are programmed to think, they assist humanity, when in fact they are re-enforcing the contracts. We constantly need to self-reflect, on all that we are doing, to ensure we are not being used.

Or, if needed, we can demand the rights to be brought in front of the regressed or the fallen councils for verification of our prerogative to cancel a contract, given that the regressed owner is gone or due to illegal trade of the contract. And then face the trial, they offer.

All the regressed worlds have legal systems and any regressed citizen has the rights to annul a contract, if the circumstances are for it. The regressed worlds live by contracts, trade and the possibility to battle for the claims or rightful ownership of something, as in a literal one-on-one combat, since the regressed races hold mixtures of insectoid, avian or reptoid genetics, which are warring in nature.

They are likewise tremendously territorial and thus, they pull all sorts of things into trial to test the claims of an opponent, the taking over of a jurisdiction etc.

This is their governance system and they live by their regressed laws and rules, albeit far from the rulesets of the progressive worlds. One could say that the laws of the regressed races are the reversed version of the progressive laws (upside-down), and that the energetic laws of the fallen worlds are the opposite (polarity) of the progressive ways.

Thus, if we do stand trial, we need to know how to defend ourselves within their rulesets and laws. Only by knowing the progressive laws and rules in full, can we dissolve the reversed and the opposite laws, governing the other worlds.

What must be observed is that the freeing work, plus the clearing and progression work, is entirely ours to do. Nobody can do it for us. Only we know what we have created, because it is stored in our template, and only we can undo it. Nobody can speak on our behalf, or undo the contracts for us. Therefore, all humans in this reality with viable genetics have to clear their own lower and upper distortion fields and connection to the distortion planes, shut down their own timelines, clear out their inserted regressed genetics as well as learning how to annul their own contracts, and subsequently undo their choices in the past cycles under these contracts.

It is the end-cycle human prerogative to fight and activate, or remain dormant and continue as part of the regressed worlds. The 5 reality zones are there for that reason. By our own efforts and the battles, we have to go through, we grow and regain our strength, knowledge and skills. The freeing work changes our energy system.

The freeing work is also done in the transformation processes of the events and the circumstances, which appear to us as we work on the timelines, by transforming the reversed or inverted events into their progressive equal.

We do the transformation work by following the Principles, the Rules and the energetic Laws of the progressive worlds in what we encounter and by working energetically with what is presented to us from the distorted timelines and the activated genetics. We erase the distortions from our timelines by doing so.

And if we cannot transform the energies and genetics into their before-timeline-event version, then we erase all and any energies and genetics to clear the timeline because it is faulty. We work our way out of the multiple distorted timelines by repairing everything that were broken, reversed and inverted by the timeline event.

The holographic manipulations to keep us within a contract, or a reversed or inverted timeline, are beyond any imagination and the regressed races, and the intra-systemics working with them, have all sorts of time altering technologies to prolong the freeing work, so we drop in energy, while doing the inner work. Most people lose sight of what they are doing in their inner work due to internal interference, so the art of staying focused and being efficient is key.

The outer manipulation to prevent us from leaving a jurisdiction, is performed by the prohibiting technologies. If interference within our reality is looked-for, then this is undertaken by various kinds of androids although, they are typically following orders from someone else higher up.[78]

The freeing work can go on for months. There are many timelines and many trickeries. Especially, if there are active contract owners in the other dimensions, because they are not eager to let go of their good production units. Secondly, most humans have difficulties believing what is going on and that they have to do the work, they have to do to gain freedom.

And most importantly: Only if the we are on top of our psychological issues and structure, our human weaknesses and working areas, can we beat and withstand the psychological warfare, we will experience to keep us within the base program and the subsequent contracts.

We have to let go of our human ways to prove our progressive rights, by declining the base program in every challenge we get. We have to demonstrate, we can do without whatever the program offers to us, to exist within this reality. This is exemplifying our free will to choose what reality, we want to participate in. And then we can create our own jurisdiction and relative reality, because as we get back to the progressive ways, the grids will sustain us in all the accurate ways to enable us to create and rebuild what we need.

---

[78] Regarding some of the androids within our world, read my book *Modern History*.

The Window of Opportunity

When a contract owner takes off, we get *the window of opportunity* to free ourselves from the old racial contract in the possession of that contract owner. But, if we miss it, the contract typically gets sold to a new regressed owner of an even worse kind. It is so, because as the higher leveled regressed races leave our system, they sell out all the contracts they have in their possessions, in order to be released from their timelines here. Not because they are cleaning up their mess and are being kind to us, but because there is the rule, that *whatever is generated, using the energies of a reality not under ownership, must remain in it, when visiting races leave.*[79]

When that happens, they are forced to offer us a chance to claim our freedom either by otherworldly fights or by tests in put-together incidents inside our reality. The incidents are orchestrated as a replay of the past – as it is possible within this non-holographic world - using situations and humans in our surroundings to do the play out. All is done to repeat the initial event that enabled the contract to be made in the first place, either under the arrangements done in our system, or by own choices done in another system to gain something.[80]

The replay of circumstances show what needs to be completed in a progressive way along with the work for us to get the contract code sequences and its technologies cleared from our energy system. The replayed circumstances annul the contract, because we energetically do it differently this time, but only if we grasp it in full, of course.

A contract is a specific coding of the energy system along with symbol insertions and technologies to uphold the programming.

---

[79] As the ISP was shut down in 2016-2017, the older regressed races having used this program, gave all of their humans a chance to get out of their segment under the ISP.
[80] Transfer of captured or contracted human template and energy systems, from the other regressed realities connected to our world, is normal.

In one case, and I have witnessed plenty of similar cases, a young man had been a gladiator in ancient Rome. He lost the fight in Rome and died. The reason why he chose to become a gladiator - because who would choose to fight against beasts and brutal men, and suffer such a horrible death - was to gain his rights as a freed man, finish off the contract with his patron and get his own a piece of land.

The energetic part, on the past timeline work, was not the death in Rome. However, that was the timeline he got presented with as if that was the clearing point. The death in Rome was just a later replay of the initial event. The trickery was to get him focused there – within our reality and in a human life - and not on the initial event in another dimension, where the contract was formed.[81]

The original circumstances for the contract were more complicated choices he had made even further back, in his own system. These old choices got him sold off to a regressed humanoid within the ancient Technocrat worlds. Given the fact, that the old worlds are engineered on holographic features, the line of events could have been undone.

He did not remember his initial choices in his own system, when the first selling took place, and thus he could not afterwards claim trickery and a subsequent re-trial to demand the contract. Hence, the window of opportunity was lost, which could have sent him into a better or at least a different trajectory with one less contract to deal with.

---

[81] All males over the course of time have got this chance within wars or different forms of battles, proving their rights to stand as a freed man. Unfortunately, without knowing the other-dimensional reasons for why they were fighting for freedom, their country or whatever. Today, males are still fighting to gain freedom, but now within the business world, as part of computer games or on the Internet. And they still do not know the reason why it is so important to them to have freedom. Females have other battles to fight. Mostly within partnerships, mating and parenting.

In essence, to get what we lost to these races, we have to repeat the scenarios and circumstances, where we lost our standings and then do the right choices in our clearing work, reencountering the initial circumstances and undo it all by following the progressive ways. It is a staged play out and we need to be on top of the game by using the Principles, Rules and Laws. Sometimes we observe the playout and at other times, we decline the offer. But, as shown above, the regressed races are not eager to return the ownership of the racial contracts, despite their unlawfulness. They would rather that the contracts, they have to leave behind when they take off, go to other regressed races to keep the contracts within their jurisdiction. Because, if they choose to come back, they can claim renewed ownership due *to omittable leave and resulting return.*

Now, nothing of this is fair and just. And it is against all the laws of the progressive human worlds, but we exist in a controlled system by the regressed, and thus we are under their rules. Humanity was sold out by fellow humans, similar to what we have seen in later times, as well as in different countries exemplifying the unjust of human rights. Not until all humans stand up for themselves, will this change. As long as humanity consent to the base program and their human ways of living, feeling and thinking, it remains so, because the base program is run by the intra-systemics and their regressed allied.

Concluding Comments
Anyways, as humans are most, nobody wants to get told they are less than perfect, and the acceptance of what we have been turned into is not easy to get to. Humans are programmed to think it is everyone else who are in the dire straits and that whatever they are, cannot be that bad because they are a good person. But what they do not get, is that it is not the person and who they are today, since most people

are nice people, but what are attached to them in the other regressed dimensions. The problem is not them, but their energy system.

The majority of humans are completely unaware of the mud-pool of regressed genetics they are infused with and that these genetics allow for interference and attachments beyond their understanding. They are not willing to accept that they are, on a daily basis, used as access points within our reality to extinguish higher order energetic settings that could lift the collective, or attack the ones that are trying to do anything that could interfere with the regressed programs. The normal human ways are destroying all the higher order energies.

Only by understanding the full scope of the invasive technologies administered by the regressed, along with the energetic and genetic modification techniques used to alter humans on an everyday basis, do humanity stand a chance.

We must get our holographic other-dimensional sight back along with our higher order capacity to be on top of what is going on, and at the same time learn how to deal with the regressed issues in a progressive manner, so that we do not fall deeper into the regressed spiral.

What we are up against are beyond all human comprehension, and we must come to terms with the work of patience this is, developing ourselves into being able to deal with a reality that beats any science fiction novel.

The human costs of doing the freeing work cannot be overlooked, but the progressive human costs of not doing it is far greater in the bigger scheme of things. And as we grow stronger, we learn to transform and transcend whatever, we might encounter. Sticking our head in the sand, knowing what we know, is a replay of the initial move done by the ancient humans. This must end. We must change history.

And not to forget. As the NGC grows stronger and the energies clear more levels of the progressive resonance fields and the holographic grids, especially if we work with the energies and the flow of the NGC, the less resistance we will get.

However, as long as we play by the tune of the base program, the work to get out is difficult because we remain, as a choice, within the regressed jurisdiction. It will remain so until the energies of the NGC hit the individual segment in 2035, if things continue as they are now.

But waiting is not an option, because further down the line, the opportunities of regaining our ancient knowledge will be gone and along with that our original progressive potentials, because the NGC clear the racial grids in 2026-2034. We will only be left with what we have become in this lifetime under the regressed protocols.

It has to be this way. Our solar system must return to the progressive worlds. The warnings about the NGC were given 2550 years ago, and humanity has not chosen to change their ways, so they are officially seen as part of the regressed worlds. The regressed use of our system is on the brink of harming the construction, mostly because of the highly invasive occupation of insectoids and androids since 2011, and thus the energies of the NGC must clear all timelines and genetics within the progressive system, connected to the regressed realities.

Humans that can must, on their own, change their energy system to follow the transit of the progressive resonance fields and racial grids. The genetic and energetic affinity cannot be circumvented. Only fully progressive humans can live in a progressive system.

And lastly, it is not about where we live, but about the ways we live, where we live. Going off-grid is not a solution. The bugs, the bees, the birds and the beasts are keeping the humanoid jurisdiction in nature.

159

The End of the Line

The regressed realities, the planetoid worlds and distorted timelines connected to our reality will in the end evaporate altogether, because of the completion of the timeline event and the incoming progressive energies of the NGC. What is left of the energies of the 3rd cycle will then disintegrate completely, as the reality grids get reset and cleared by the NGC. This is what leads to the cold dark universe in the future, because what is left after the progressive grids are gone, is nothing but old cycle depleted energy and an emptied out DE1.

There is a possibility that the remaining regressed races choose an extraction before this happens and perform a complete grid and field removal of their jurisdictions, transferring their inserted grids to their own worlds. If that solution is chosen, all that is connected to their racial grids and jurisdictions will be transported to the regressed realities, since what were spawned using their grids technically never were part of this world, but their inserted grids. That includes human templates and genetics under the regressed contracts or part of their grids, having been engineered using the racial grids belonging to the regressed.

Human templates and genetics that are pulled into such worlds, are not able to reunite with the progressive worlds later on. So, losing the small scale favors we have gained in the present-day world are worth losing, compared to what we will face if we do not change our human ways. Unless of course, it is a preferred choice to remain regressive and a wish to join the regressed races. That is a human prerogative. So is making the choice of quitting and do the evaporation process.

It is time to add the last piece, i.e. *the prohibiting technologies* to the equation, and in that deepening our technological understanding.

160

The Prohibiting Technologies

The basic idea, of polluting and distorting the original energy system with the three lower fields, was to secure that no pillar human within the base program could interact with the overall rings of progression and, in that way, surpass the regressed programs.

It was done this way, because all pillar humans – from our system or from other systems - have the power to recover and regain the knowledge of how to progress correctly, both as an individual and on a collective level.

Thus, any present-day human with viable original genetics holds the knowledge of how to obtain the information and capacities to work appropriately with the reality energies and the progression rings in a productive and governing way, and he or she knows how to use that knowledge for the highest good of the many.

However, to ensure that no former pillar human could fully activate, the regressed races made further insurances, because it is possible to clear out the connection to the lower distortion planes quite easily by the correct clearing work and by developing new sets of behavior and attitudes following the higher order choices shown in the Principles, the Rules and the Laws along with rearranging everyday life to exist outside the base program in our own jurisdictions.

Meditation techniques, as in silent self-observation, can be utilized to observe how the three lower fields operate energetically in us. Then in a more active meditation, using creative imagination along with the

HAL Basic Energy Work, can be used to transform the base program layers in us. The higher order work is done in the clearing work and dealing with what comes our way from the timelines, we bring to life by activating the genetics in our energy system and by that, the match on the timelines. The freeing work follows the clearing work. Different techniques apply to the different stages of our inner work but they would all come online, by themselves, if it were not for the prohibiting technologies.

To prevent the natural progression out of the regressed state from happening, the prohibiting technologies were invented and attached to all pillar humans, to ensure that if a human managed to get out of the distortion energies, the prohibiting technologies would kick in.

The prohibiting technologies will remain attached to humans, as long as the regressed races are present and working in our system. Each regressed faction has their own sets of suppression and prohibiting technologies, and they are all built according to their genetic markers, the energy structures of their grids, their purposes and what they do here. Thus, there are not two sets of technologies that are fully equal.

The Detecting Alarm Systems
If any attempt is done within the regressed areas to clear the lower fields or if similar actions are taken, which can be seen as a threat to the continuation of the programs and control systems running these jurisdictions, an instant alarm goes off. Following the alarm, incoming drones or cubes – often three to four to get every angle of the energy system – then run scans of the complete energy system to spot what is going on.

According to the field scans and the diagnostics, supplementary holographic symbols are inserted into the fields to keep the genetic fragments working according to their initial programming, along with additional prohibiting technologies to guarantee a renewed growth of any cleared energetic parasites and attachments. Anything is done to ensure continuance of the regressed state in a human, and it happens automatically.

Additional supplements of regressed genetics - if these have been cleared out or transformed – are inserted into the lower order fields to patch-up and renew the distortion levels of the ego structure and the emotional and mental fields. A resetting of the brain and a mental field wiping are also normal, to remove the memories of the clearing work priorly done and the knowledge that was gained. If the patch-up is not sufficient enough to keep the lockdown running, the entire field system is pulled in during sleep and recalibrated, cloned or redone in all ways possible to remove the achieved level of freeing work.

The re-cloning work, mostly done by androids, is done in other-dimensional realities under the regressed races.

The semi-organic to fully androids can peep in from time to time, if they are in charge of maintaining the technologies connected to the surface area human. Again, most of the semi-organic androids are working under a specific faction and not really working on their own. Unless of course, they have been left behind by their faction and then the androids believe they have their own human project going on. These are the worst androids to deal with, because machines cannot discern what is the best way to maintain a human subject, and they have no one to correct them. Machines think like machines, and they do not understand that a human is organic and cannot be patched up or fixed by getting the interior shifted out.

In spite of the attempted intervention from the higher order worlds on a systemic level and the incoming NGC, if a human is living within the regressed jurisdictions and if that human is not working actively to prove that he or she wants out, that human is technically seen as consenting to the regressed programs going on in the area where he or she lives, and then there is nothing the councils can do.

A progressive human that wants his or her freedom, after having been in oblivion for ages, must do the work to regain his or her memories and full capacity. Nobody will do that for us, because both the ancient human races sold us off and the lineages descending from these races have continued to accept the original deals, despite the attempts from the higher order councils to undo them in a vast number of meetings, where the power elite was attending.[82]

Here in the completion cycle, humans must take a stand and choose in which reality zone, they belong. If they choose to live in the regressed zone, they must prove that they are not consenting to what is going on there. That they are in that zone for a purpose under the NGC, and not to continue the regressed ways, but to clear and reestablish the progressive human ways in these areas. Everything else will be seen as a consent to the regressed ways.

A progressive human must prove that he or she is not consenting to the prohibiting technologies, the ancient contracts and the unlawful ownership of a progressive human and the ways the regressed are doing their businesses here.

---

[82] The in-the-know humans, running our world via their business and governmental structures, will lose everything when the grids turn progressive. They will have to stand trial in front of the progressive councils and face the transgression rate of their deeds and the extended time they have chosen to keep up the exploitation of fellow humans, they could have brought back to the progressive worlds. The confrontation with the power elite will happen in the racial activation and cleanup phase of the NGC, and we are already seeing the build up for that scenario.

How the Prohibiting Technologies Work

The prohibiting and control technologies within the human fields are a huge problem, because they work in a shrewd way: Whenever one level is cleared, the next level of lockdown technologies will drop into the three lower fields, distorting the perception field with new false visual and auditory inputs. The new level leads the work off track and into new false reality setups and ideas of what is important to do.

When we succeed in shutting down a timeline and clear out the genetics, the timeline we are freed from gets relooped and then we are reinserted into the new, by rearranging our template and energy system during the night. We are inserted into an earlier point on the timeline, but now with a dissimilar trajectory and we are technically on a new branch. The new insertion point and the rearrangement of our template, create new branches on the timeline and our freeing work is nullified. Theoretically, the work we did is still valid, but since we are now on a new branch, we do not get the effects of our freeing work. That work is left on the other branch, we were removed from.

Overall, the prohibiting technologies work in the same way as a house of cards. As long as the human is situated in the base program and does not do any real attempts to activate the higher order energy system, the lower order fields function as they are supposed to; the lower fields generate the normal human experience and induce the sense of what is important to do in this world to keep up a certain way of living, a relationship, a business or whatever seems important on a psychological level. Nothing else is perceived or understood.

But if a person wants to activate the higher order energy system, the counteractions are set in motion and the house of cards begins to collapse. When one level is cleared out correctly, two things happen: 1) the patch-up countermeasures kick in, as described above, and 2) at the same time the next sub-level of the regression spiral and its distorted rings of reality get activated, overflowing us with additional regressed genetics to deal with and the new prohibiting technologies belonging to that sub-level of the regressed reality.

Not only are we then dealing with the regressed counteraction mechanics of the cleared level but also the new unknown regressed technologies, symbols, attachments and energetic parasites and how to handle these.

It unfolds this way, because the regressed spiral follows the original progression spiral dynamics. When one cycle is done and completed in the progression worlds, and the higher order genetics and energies are achieved, the next cycle begins on a higher level of the progression spiral along with what we have accomplished.

In the regression spiral the dynamics are the same, but in a reverse manner, pulling us further down. The regressed races have been using our own technologies against us by reverse engineering them to work in the opposite or reversed ways. Once we get that, it is easy to deal with the dynamics of the regressed spiral.

Consequently, as long as we do not take the time to learn about the prohibiting technologies, we stand no real chance in our activation process, but if we endure the challenges and get to a level of higher order perception, it is possible to remove the regressed holographic technologies, since the consciousness genetics are part of all forms of higher order technologies, including the regressed technologies.

The weakness of the regressed technologies is the very same thing, they are using to control us, which is the inserted genetic fragments. Given the fact, that we are infused with the genetics of the regressed humanoid races, we can backtrack from the inserted genetics and into their technologies to take these fully out. It is possible to learn and an achievable procedure. All programs have back-doors and that go for the inserted genetics as well, because they are engineered. What is used to access us and control us, we can use to access their timelines and take out all the technologies, controlling us from there.

Most of the genetic fragments in our energy system are replications. They are highly infused with memory imprints from the contributors, making it difficult for us to discern between what are our memories or if they are part of the regressed humanoids. Some of the imprints are utterly false and created memories. But once we get through that confusion, we can learn to clear the genetic fragments of their visual and energetic content. Following this, we can read the information they hold, where they come from and then track the linkup to the technologies, they are part of. When we have the coding information, we can clear out the genetics upholding the technologies by using our higher order capacities. After having dealt with the technologies, we can clear the timelines the technologies were positioned within, and then shut down all projects on that timeline that are not functioning for the highest good of the many.

All progressive humans can work with genetic coding and know how to dissolve and amplify genetics. These skills are part of the 1-7 pillar.

The Semi-Organic Parasites
The prohibiting technologies always involve some sort of 4th and 5th dimensional semi-organic parasite. While the energetic parasites are the unfortunate consequence of wrongful use of genetics, the semi-organic parasites are deliberately inserted and they act as *the worm in the middle* between the organic form and the attached technology.

The 4th and 5th dimensional semi-organic parasites are hooked up to prohibiting technologies, situated in adjacent regressed realities, and thus technically not part of our solar system.

The 4th and 5th dimensional semi-organic parasites are similar in composition to e.g. the gut and skin parasites we hold on a microbial level. As the 4th and 5th dimensional semi-organic parasites are pulled out from our energy system, what appears are enlarged versions of the microbial lifeforms, we hold. It is so, because the microbes in our body, including the mitochondria, were inserted as part of the human reengineering to enable the 4-5D semi-organic parasites to bridge the human body to the prohibiting technologies. The microbes within our body and the larger 4th and 5th dimensional semi-organic parasites live in a symbiotic relationship and they are equally producing regressed energy in us.[83]

Via the 4th and 5th dimensional semi-organic parasitic linkup[84] and the reengineering of us, we are easily mind and emotionally steered, because the environment in us is not ours alone, so to speak.

We respond to the changes in the microbes and what is made to unfold into our energy system from the regressed timelines, through the prohibiting technologies. In many ways, the distortion planes are the result of this energetic and the semi-organic parasitic linkup. They make us distort everything. But at the same time, the 4-5D semi-organic parasites force us to a high degree of psychological insight to circumvent the inner manipulation of how we feel and think. We can

---

[83] Most human illnesses stem from the microbes in our body.

[84] The semi-organic parasites have names according to their function. There are the Deceivers, the Deceptors, the Procures, the Falsifiers to name a few. They alter the endocrine glands with their enzymes to make us feel or think in a specific way. The insertion of the parasites is done through symbols, making the parasites grow in a specific way. It can also be done by middle domain humans regressed into humanoid ants accessing our field from the 4th dimension or via transfer from another human, having an 4D ant attached to them. The ants carry the genetic spores, to create a parasite, on their back and when entering our field, they shed off these spores.

learn to sense when they shoot off their enzymes to affect our glands, brain and nervous system. A higher sensitivity and acknowledgement of what is going on in our body is crucial to that.

So, we can use that to our advantage in our progression work, if we accept that we are always up against hidden energies and *powers* in us and around us.

This knowledge forces us to work with the Principles, the Rules and the Laws in their correct ways, because we know, we cannot trust our human ways or what we have learned inside the base program to be the correct ways of being a "good human."

At the end of the day, we are not only fighting against all that has been done to us, but also what we did that led to it. Timeline work is a work done in the past cycles, presented to us in present era and the probable futures, our inner work will lead to. And a good approach to all we are to go through is to not view ourselves as victims.

Victimization disempowers and takes away our strength in the heart field to do the work. If we get too emotional, the parasites will get the better of us. Humanity made it possible to get to this collective state of existence by their choices. We can make it possible to undo these choices.

We have to remember that most of the choices were all made for the right reasons, unless we got too infected and thus made them for all the wrong reasons, but in the dealing with the regressed human races and the humanoids that sprung from these lineages, we could not have foreseen what would happen and subsequently, we did not act appropriately. Let us not repeat that mistake to the incoming energies of the NGC.

The Difficulty of Our System

In the freeing and the clearing work, we are to take into consideration that the obstacles to free our system are different compared to other human systems who have been or are dominated by the regressed races. Most of the other realities, affected by the timeline event and thus made vulnerable for a takeover, were altered into technological hive-mind driven realities, controlling the population that way.

This did not happen in our system, because we were part of the first solar system to implement the 6-12 pillar and in a system run by the original technologies of the Ancient Ones. In our solar system, the progressive humans had a high degree of self-governance. On top of that, they had advanced abilities to work with the dynamics of their reality, developing their energy systems and reengineer genetics. This level of advanced progression demanded a complex energetic setup and the 6-12 pillar organic vessels were engineered in a different way, compared to the vessels of humans in other progressive worlds, to accommodate for the 6-12 pillar developmental programs. Due to our level of advancement and the construction of our system, the 6-12 pillar setup would not allow for a technological overtaken system. Hence, the prohibiting technologies, to keep us in the loop of control, had to be done in a dissimilar manner to avoid the core facilities and the Workstations to reboot. Also, the regressed races had to work around the protective fail-safe mechanism, which was implemented to safeguard the irreplaceable technologies of the Ancient Ones.

If the fail-safe mechanism were to activate, due to absence of any lifeforms in alignment with the 6-12 pillar developmental programs, it would initiate the sequences to run a complete reset of our system and it would then be impossible for the regressed races to exist and work here. So, the regressed races used the turned pillar humans to gain access to the administration facilities, from where they could modify programs and outposts to fit the humanoid genetics. Without the help from the turned pillar humans, the regressed races could not have accessed the facilities due to lack of genetic affinity.

The fail-safe mechanism is one of the reasons why humans on our planet are still in an organic form, looking as we do – although very reengineered - and having a sort of individual mind, along with a world that kind of looks progressive, however entirely built upon the energies of the timeline event. All lifeforms here are made to imitate a system of progression with a balanced use of technology.

These circumstances add to a more complicated work on all levels of our system, compared to other systems, along with the fact that we have to catch up with the consequences of the NGC and having no clue of what is in store for us.[85]

The incoming energies of the NGC will make all energetic layers of our system come to life in various unpredictable ways, affecting the lifeforms on our planet, in equally unpredictable ways.[86]

And to fuel further concerns, because of the restoring of the core facilities due to the NGC and the reestablishing of the progressive reality fields and racial grids around us, the regressed technologies, along with the semi-organic to fully energetic parasites and so forth will eventually stop working, break down and undergo an evaporation process. If humans are not on top of that clearing process, they will undergo a similar breakdown process energetically and organically.

---

[85] At least the humanoids, although being insectoid, avian, reptoid or mammal, have their racial memories intact and the advanced technological understanding. But they have lost all knowledge of the progression worlds and that there is another way.
[86] All lifeforms on our planet have this extra dimensional layout. Animals, insects, birds and reptiles have their other-dimensional archetypes attached to them and when dealing with the changes of our system, this has to be taken into consideration.

The Rehabilitation Zone

When we progress and clear our energy system of distortion and are able to hold the higher order energies to balance out all that comes our way, we *can* leave behind the intrusion and the constant attacks from the regressed races. These intimidation games are done to keep us in their jurisdiction by lowering our energies. It is not easy, but it is possible but again, it depends on our choices and where we choose to live, and whom we choose to be surrounded by.

As long as we choose to live in a regressed jurisdiction and to be surrounded by family members, partners and friends who are not doing the work, we will remain voluntarily in a warzone.

It is so, because we cannot fully change it into our jurisdiction. To completely do that, we have to have committed humans around us. We can change the energies in our home to our standards, but only if the entire household is doing the work. Otherwise it is a mixed zone. The laws of energetic and genetic affinity stand, and the interference from our surroundings will be higher than what we can maintain of cleared and progressive energies. We will continuously have to work to keep the balance, and we will constantly be affected by our fellow humans, not doing the work and thus choosing to remain regressed.

Nevertheless, at some point we can choose to instigate and begin the mandatory energy work to enter the rehabilitation zones in the slightly, for the purpose, altered progressive dimensions.[87]

The rehabilitation zone is engineered as a partly regressed, partly progressive energetic space, made this way because we are that too.

---

[87] Going off grid with this understanding, is different than believing that going off-grid alone will make things better. They will not. But at least the interference will be less.

It was actually created 2550 years ago, but not many have been using it because the original knowledge of how to get there got lost in the deception maneuvers of the regressed humans inside our reality.[88]

Plus, most humans that got the offer 2550 years ago would not leave behind their families, friends and partners or their everyday life. Most thought they could withstand the interference and still work to become part of the progressive grids. Well, both the inner and outer history have taught us differently.

Within the rehabilitation zone – which is an inner energetic space and thus, we are still in our human vessel and living within a surface area - we can transform the remaining other-dimensional regressed genetics, and reassemble our fragmented template. It will not make the transition work easier, but at least we are energetically coupled to a non-hostile density environment, as we sojourn in and out of our distorted higher timelines of the past, completing the transition work we need to do to get out of the regression spiral. And yet again, at some point our outer life has to change completely, if we want to go all the way and get connected to the rehabilitation zone.

The Final Remarks

Although the core facilities are rebooting and resetting to follow the upgrading of our universe, the energetic levels of the entire human population will remain within the collective distortion fields for a long time, due to the absence of general knowledge of how to clear the remaining timelines etc. In other words; the distorted collective fields of humanity will continue to fuel the lower order energies in the DE1 sector of our reality and with that, make the overall progression work difficult. As long as we remember that, and that the inner work is a

---

[88] The regressed races have rehabilitation zones too, mimicking "safe-zones" when in fact these energetic realities are just another incarceration space full of holographic niceties, similar to the idea of a heaven, an afterlife or a new earth.

work of patience, we can go a long way. Step by step we will do the needed transition work.

Humans with viable genetics will strive for changes. They can make all the important adjustments in their lives to face the challenges of the future in appropriate ways, along with dealing with the processes of change on a collective level, as our reality undergoes its transition.

In the upcoming years, the changes will be seen here and there. The effects of the activation and cleanup and the segregation of the viable grids, preparing these for a reuniting with the progression worlds, are becoming noticeable in different ways. And as the dynamics of the NGC resetting multiplies over time, the effects of the activation and the cleanup of the reality grids and the racial grids will be felt on a collective level and on an individual level in more profound ways.

The future challenges within our world will sooner or later lead to changes in the preferred lifestyle of humanity, along with the removal of the archaic forms of businesses. What is in store for us will lead to development of new technologies to meet up with the new demands from and in our world.

The question is, despite the collective changes in overall behavior, if the general population will return to the progressive human ways or remain as part of the DE1. An entirely technological-mechanical advanced human world is not what the NGC brings about nor is it a progressive world.

The only possible way for us to catch the waves of changes and the incoming higher order density energies, is to do the needed clearing work to remove all the inserted regressed holographic technologies, regressed genetics and parasites, and their code systems. And then, of course, change our human ways, to repeat it one more time.

174

We are to create our own jurisdiction, i.e. a private field within the collective field to handle the collective energies, using the knowledge of the relative reality and the progression spiral to ensure that we can catch up with the NGC energies and not be overtaken by any outer interfering circumstances. We must arrange ourselves in ways, inner and outer, that are able to adjust to the incoming NGC energies on an everyday basis, securing income and real-life circumstances to be able to adapt and change, when needed, including preparing ourselves for the demands of the higher order systems and the progressive worlds. And then we will do what we can, the best way we can.

Also, we do this work as the first of many for the highest good of the many. We choose to live this way so that the innovative attempts of what it means to be human can be exemplified into the collective consciousness field as well as into the world.

Our world needs pioneering methods of existence and different approaches to utilization of natural resources. We are manifesting the progressive ideas by being it, living and by expressing it. All changes need role models, and implementation of changes take years of work. It is a prerequisite that there are people leading the way, to enable any shift of reality and seeding of new ideas.

Therefore, we live the HAL philosophy to that level of perfection, we find suitable for us. Leaving behind the base program does not imply that we go rouge or become intolerable citizens; it means that we have learned to live in the physical world and have mastered it to the degree, we need to enable us to exist in both the lower and the higher order worlds.

We still have a foot in the lower order system, so we can behave appropriately in all situations. We still pay our tax and we uphold the human laws to the dot. We do the attempt to have as little energetic impact as possible on other humans that do not want the progressive changes. It is a valid choice not wanting to progress.

We cannot impose progression onto other humans. As we learn about relative reality in action, we will see that is it not necessary to change other humans, but only to progress what we are and what we want to exemplify into the world, by creating a jurisdiction of energy.

That will generate the needed changes around us to attract the people, we need in our life to make our segment work accordingly to the Principles, the Rules and the Laws.

In essence; there will be clusters of new approaches to what it means to be human, manifested into the collective racial field, and if these clusters are viable and serve the highest good of the many, they will become the general way of living. If the clusters of expressed life are not viable, they will manifest their cycle and then die out. It has always been that way.

So, no need to worry about other humans. They are free to make their choices. We are not to choose what is best for them, since we do not know what their history is, in this life and beyond. And they are living out their cycles in this reality, as they know best for the time being. Later on, when the energies of our solar system have changed, there will be a need of adaptation on all levels of our reality - human and world - but nature is wise and the core energies will take care of that. Circumstances will teach humans what they need to change, to be able to follow the original incoming reality energies, emitted from the higher order worlds.

We are the forefront, and all of our work is paving the way. And just to make it clear – the forefront makes all of the mistakes and gets hit the worst; so that is the reality we enter into by choosing to be the first of many for the highest good of the many.

With the bigger picture in place, the historical background and the understanding of the NGC, it is time to clear some concepts.

In the free communities we have platforms where Spheres holding
the Living Ancient Wisdom are free for all to connect to.
The Spheres are living energy since they are connected directly to
the core domains and the Ancient Ones.

We gather around, some standing others sitting in silent
meditation, and listen to the knowledge being handed to us via
the CD center in the head. The platform is placed out in the open
and all free communities I have visited have a high degree of
nature and simple living.

How to Use the HAL Books

So, how to use the 2014-2017 HAL books in the years to come?

Although most of the information in the 2014-2017 HAL books is not actively in play on a collective scale due to changes in our reality the last 5 years, the information is still valid because of the individual segments of reality, everybody is moving through in their own pace.

The template and timeline work depend on the individual and the work follows its own sequences, for the reason that the chiasm and what timelines, each person is working on in the clearing work, are both part of the individual history as well as of the collective history.

The timeline work will define, which parts of history each person is seeing and working through in the inner perception field. Timeline work – moving backwards and forwards in time – thus depends on the genetics in the template, and which timelines they are integrated into. That will define which sections of the collective history that are perceived and are to be worked with on a personal level. Only pieces of the genetics stuck on timelines, we did not complete correctly, are to be worked with. The rest will not be shown to us. Therefore, the goal of the HAL books is to provide the missing pieces of the overall picture, as we encounter our personal section of that timeline.

In that way, the information given in the books is historically key, and plays an important role in knowing our collective history, as we work through our individual piece of the general history to clear our failures on the timelines in the past, change our ways in the present and clear out the energies of the futures, these mistakes can lead to. Consequently, the 2014-2017 HAL books are to be seen as individual and collective frames of reference, so we can piece together the full picture. The HAL books additionally explain the foundational concepts of reality and give the needed background to understand what we are to work with, in our individual timeline work, since each and one of us carry the energetic remnants, genetics and prohibiting technologies from the regressed races in our template and energy systems.[89]

The here-present HAL Philosophy book adds the remaining and updated pieces of the progression, transformation and clearing work, and why we should do it. It paves the way into our future work under the NGC.

Learning from History
Therefore, the remainders of the regressed races and their operations here - energetically, consciously and technologically – do define the history of our race and it is lurking in the background, when we begin the lifelong transition and progression work to be able to perceive the higher order realities again.

Remember; the ones that have not learned from their personal history are bound to repeat their mistakes, because the lessons that had to be learned on the timelines of our reality, will be repeated in alternate versions until what needs to be learned, is understood and integrated as knowledge. And then different choices can be made, altering the course of the future. The future only changes, if we change our ways.

The overall goal of the template and timeline work is to generate the best possible futures for all. This work follows the highest purity rate, the highest standards and the highest progression rate for all possible future races. If we have done deeds in the past that prevent this, we

---

[89] In the 2014-2017 books it is explained that we have 5 energy systems fitting the 5 tiers – LPRF1 to LPRF5 - of our reality. These are part of the old human projects and are to be fully cleared via our template and timeline work.

have to correct our mistakes by transforming whatever enforced the wrongdoings. We have to create new timeline choices, utilizing the holographic features of the timelines under the Principles, the Rules and the Laws, and according to the original standards of our system. Otherwise, we will be stuck with the outcome of our failed choices, because only the seeder can remove what were seeded in the past - including the choices done under manipulation - and only the creator knows the energetic combination and coding. Hence, only the creator can undo what he or she has created. And that means us.

The knowledge of how to work appropriately with all energies, reality and our genetics, to follow the standards of our system, are encoded into our template. We learn how to reprogram the code sheets by our repeated work on the timelines, unfolding their content to us within the holographic projections our perception field produces for us. Once we remember how to reprogram our code sheets, no further timeline work is needed.

In other words: Our lack of understanding of what we are and can do, will hold us back, until we have understood all the information hidden in the many timelines connected to our template and energy system.

All templates and energy systems are part of the progression spiral that drives our solar system and the process of progression, we were to undertake and failed. We are bound by the Law of the Cycles; what was seeded in one cycle has to be completed in the same cycle, or within another, before we can move on. And we need to move on both as individuals and as a race. We need to progress.

So, where do we go from here?
As the first thing, we need to change how we think.

Letting Go of Outdated Beliefs

The approach of the HAL Philosophy is the development of the higher awareness *outside* all ancient and contemporary spiritual, esoteric or religious concepts, we have access to today.

Even though the HAL Philosophy has similarities with the ancient philosophical systems, the basic notion in the HAL work is that most ancient ideas of the other realities are either distorted or outdated no matter how much they are refined to fit modern spiritual, esoteric or religious concepts.

It is so, because the ideas, used in the ancient teaching systems, were developed by humans some 7500 to 100 years ago within secret or priestly fraternities, and - not to forget - these fraternities saw the males as the only true practitioners of the secret knowledge. Females were to assist or were prohibited from accessing any knowledge at all, whether we talk about the Hindu-guru practitioners or within the Eastern and Western secret fraternities. Although, there were female practitioners found as equals within the ancient Buddhist schools.[90] And of course, this changed in the later 1800, where we find several female practitioners of the ageless wisdom. In fact, there was a rise of female leaders within the secret fraternities.[91]

And yet again, not that the HAL Philosophy appraises these. The ideas, the people who practiced it and what they built energetically of distortion and deception, serve no purpose for humanity today.[92]

---

[90] Women in Buddhism https://en.wikipedia.org/wiki/Women_in_Buddhism
[91] https://en.wikiquote.org/wiki/The_Ageless_Wisdom_Teachings
[92] As it is said: "Let the dead be dead and let the living take care of the living." We have to stop worshipping the religions of the dead, the sciences of the dead and the politics of the dead. Our present-day world system is built upon death and not life.

And finally, the majority of the ancient mystery schools had their traditions from secret teaching systems dating back to ancient India, Egypt or Mesopotamia, which in turn had their secret traditions from the priesthood of the last stages of Atlantis.[93]

At that time, Atlantis had become a world nobody deserved to be part of. And subsequently, there is no need to continue the Atlantean teaching systems either. It has to be remembered why any teaching system lingers on and who benefits from it energetically.

It is equally important to acknowledge that the ancient teaching systems were established within cultures with a dissimilar look upon the world including what a human was, its purpose and why it even existed. All humans were under the laws and the will of the gods.[94]

The ancient worlds were organized in societies upheld by human division and hierarchical structures, exercising suppression of males and females in different systems of slavery. Not that things are better now, i.e. we are still bound to the functions as breeders and workers, but the point being here is that present-day appraisal of the ancient systems serves no purpose because, no matter how much we polish these ancient systems, the foundational energy is wrong.

Goodbye Religion

Religion is no better, since the Abrahamic religions - flourishing to this day - stem from the identical ancient structures and period of time. Women were not allowed into the Jewish temple, but were to stay in

---

[93] The Atlantis the HAL Philosophy refer to, is not the Atlantis of Plato, although the line of origin he referred to in a way is correct. However, Plato´s ideas of Atlantis was made to exemplify his version of what human society could become. About Plato´s Atlantis https://en.wikipedia.org/wiki/Atlantis

[94] And the work within the fraternities was about creating a connection to these gods and serve them directly, as their empowered liaison within this world, to ground the will of the gods amongst men. The knowledge was about how to become worthy in the eyes of the gods by rising up in degrees of powers. In essence, the mass was to worship the gods within religion, and the fraternities were to do the will of the gods.

the women's courtyard veiled, silent and hidden away. They were not permitted to address any religious matters within the temple, or later on, within the synagogues.

In early Christianity, women were not permitted to contribute to the get-togethers either, being the offshoot of Judaism as it was. They had to stay veiled in the assemblies, to avoid tempting and drawing in the fallen angels.[95]

However, it was a common trait in the ancient worlds to perceive females as lesser and males as the highest ranked humans. Within all levels of society of the ancient worlds, women were seen as lower ranked humans and, in many ways, they are still seen as such. Though Christians today think they have grown out of this bias, the fact of the matter is that the root of it still lingers on in the church of Christ.[96]

As it is with the ancient lineages of humans, which we are bound to by heritage and partake in due to our genetics, we are also bound to the lineages of ideas and energies of the thought forms, we choose to believe in and perceive the world from. Present-day humans have a long way to go to reach energetic equality in race, gender and skin color. And letting go of religion is part of this.

The Soul

The idea of a soul was created within ancient Greek philosophies and then transferred into the Abrahamic religions, some more prone to the idea than others. The notion of the soul was further developed within the esoteric and spiritual teaching systems in the late 1800's, along with selected bits and pieces from the prehistoric Egyptian and Indian teaching systems, neatly brewed together into a new form of personal development using the ancient energy techniques.

---

[95] Paul addressed this in his letters, probably referring to the book of Genesis and the Nephilim, or perhaps the Watchers from the book of Enoch. Look it up.
[96] Actually, it is more the church of Peter: https://en.wikipedia.org/wiki/Saint_Peter

All with a specific purpose of course. And that purpose has not been for the betterment of humanity. If it had, we would be in a different place now, right?

All in all, we need to look upon our systems of thought from new perspectives, and not mindlessly repeat and replicate the ideas of the ancient worlds. Just because it is old, does not make it better.

Goodbye Gods

Of course, the idea of the human being composed of different levels of energy still stands, but the religious and spiritual paradigms, into which the dynamics and methods of the human energy system have been interpreted, have been twisted into non-empowering dynamics, as well as an approach that places the power of the individual into the hands of one or more deities, making the human a godly made creation, expected to be subservient, a slave and not the progressive caretaker, we ideally are supposed to be. Humans are to develop the reality they are part of and not some outer force in another realm.

All forms of religions and spiritual belief systems, which allow for and give away our power and responsibility to higher forces, are to be left behind. It is time to become a responsible world citizen, doing the progression work to develop what we are as well as our reality, and not behaving like children, awaiting instructions from absent superior forces.

The HAL Philosophy does not include any god or gods. It only operates with the regressed or inverted humanoid races thinking they are gods. And these races have functioned as such within our world for a long time.[97] It is time to lift the veil and see them for what they are.

---

[97] By making humans worship the ones, that had no allowances to be here, as gods. This worship gave them the green card into our reality.

A New Cultural Mindset

The ways we have been utilizing our world's resources, to explore our reality and ourselves, have only gotten us so far.

Throughout the industrial age, humanity has grown into a lower order mechanical mindset, with the focus on technology over human progression and because of that, our ways of thinking are still, aside from our lesser technological endeavors, primitive and self-oriented. We need to do a reality check on our self-perception and definitions of what we are, because contrary to what most people think, we have not progressed a lot in the last many thousands of years, if we are to view our progress on a scale of consciousness. Most contemporary humans believe that our race has evolved, but that only stands to reason by a comparison to the idea that humans have evolved from an apelike hominid some 210,000 years ago. Or by seeing the older civilizations as part of the stone age, the bronze age etc., of which none of these labels accurately reflect the civilizations at the time, their entrepreneurship, knowledge and inventions.

It is so, because the interpretation of the skulls and bones found in the ground are anthropological biased. The ideas of homo sapiens date back to the 1800's, where the scientific communities were eager to prove the standards of the Western civilizations as the preferred ideals for all humans to follow.

Anthropology was used to enforce the Western world as the peak of all human civilizations and because of that gave allowances for them to colonize other countries. It paved the way to take over and destroy functional other-cultural human societies and forced them to be part of the Western world structure. Not as equals, but as lesser humans and within new rounds of slavery, and with settings probably far worse than that of the ancient worlds.

All human sciences need to be brought up-to-date to encompass new equality and human rights perspectives. We need to by-pass the antiquated interpretation paradigms founded by *the dead white men* of the past, and remove all of their ideas from mainstream sciences.

Ending the Age of Technological Wonders
Thus, the human endeavors and civilization are measured in the light of contemporary technology and sciences, but the true fact is that we have devolved. Our mindset and our ways of living are disastrous, not only to ourselves but to all lifeforms. We are killing ourselves, other lifeforms and destroying our world by what we have become and the ways we live.

Over the last 200 years, a lot of determination has been put into producing technologies, mechanical innovations, and the sciences to accommodate these, with the goal of exploitation of other lifeforms along with an overuse of planetary resources. Far too few innovations have been focused on technologies and sciences that would preserve our planet, its resources and the continuation of the human race.

And it is odd, is it not, considering that there are so many good-hearted people out there, and so many attempts to make our world better? So, why are we not improving? Why do humans not live up to their full potentials in a continued evolution?

It is time to understand why we have become like grasshoppers, ruining our own world and figure out what we need to do to change that. In spite of our attempts to develop as a joint human race, we have failed, seen from a higher perspective of human evolution.

We need higher order approaches towards everything we know about what it means to be human, to all known sciences, to our world and to our understanding of energy.[98]

---

[98] Sciences, technologies and innovations are lightyears away from the technologies, we could have invented, if humanity had chosen differently. These technologies are part of the original human knowledge base, implemented into the human template and genetics.

We Are Not the Peak

We must move beyond the idea that humanity is more civilized today than the older versions of our race. That we exemplify higher social and psychological skills than in the ancient world. To some degree we have; we do not have gladiator games or burn humans on the stake (today, there are computer games or movies with the same themes) but in terms of social and psychological skills, we have not advanced that much. Ancient texts from the everyday life of the common man and woman in the ancient world, show us this. Unfortunately, there is not much left for us to work with, but the few findings are enough to show us that humanity has not evolved that much on the social and psychological scale.

Of course, we have rearranged the outer world with technology and mechanical aid that runs on electricity. However, that might also be challenged in the future, as we begin to interpret the findings in the ground in their accurate light. From this, we can dig deeper and discover that the ancient world had inventions, we can only dream of today. Lots to be revealed if these mechanical items surface from the ground.

Our belief of our superiority only stands, because we have been conditioned to believe in a historical setup, which puts us in the top of all human evolution. The truth is that we are at the bottom of what a human can become. The technology we currently use is far behind the holographic-consciousness technologies, our world is based upon. And yet again, these advanced technologies are in use today, just not by humans within our world. Contrary, naturally, to how it was in the original earth colonies, aka the outposts under the pillar projects. [99]

---

[99] Why not see the human remains, found in excavations as being part of advanced human races? It stands to reason, considering the extremely high-tech smooth cut of granite stones we find in e.g. Machu Picchu, and other similar stone cuttings found in all ancient cities, reused in later building structures of the following civilizations.

We live in a lower order level of our reality and our technologies reflect that. We need to get our higher order consciousness back, so that we can reconnect to the higher density layers of our system and the higher order technologies and from that, do the correct evolution of our world and our race.

A Mechanically Based Future – No Thanks
We do the progression journey to set goals that ensure a progressive, knowledgeable and empathic foundation of a continued human race. It is up to us to choose a different future and to avoid enforcing a DE1 future, consisting of artificial intelligence and semi-automatic device systems, global terraforming industries under private contractors and encompassed weather modification technologies.

We do not need a future made up of human-to-machine interface technologies, augmented or virtual realities run by self-developing AI matrices, holographic brain-induction and modification technologies to amplify the synaptic neural network.

We do not need any 3D organ production using a combination of microbiology and nanotubes upgraded with enhanced DNA from non-human sources, generating hybrid humans as well as leading to the development of the semi-organic clones, androids and robotoids. All of which is in the making.

DNA Engineering – No Thanks
Similarly, until humans understand the full scope of what DNA truly is, we must stand against human DNA engineering, reduction, selection

---

Plus, the fact that the surface and crust of our planet is being turned inside-out all the time. That makes it difficult to date the deeper layers correctly. A lot of evidence is also lost because of that. And the simple fact that most of these technologies are in the 4th dimension.

and similar approaches, which lead to an unnatural tampering with the human genome. From the belief that DNA editing can guarantee a perfect human and can remove all diseases.

If humanity accept these ideas, they allow for private unwatched industries to interfere with the human genome. Not for the highest good of the many to progress our race, but for the good of the few that are technically speaking, dysfunctional. It is controversial to state that, but perhaps there is a reason for the dysfunctional DNA? Such as a depleting energy system and non-viable consciousness genetics?

Besides, these industries support a continued genetic harvesting and exploitation of humanity, here and beyond. It cannot be allowed. Illness is produced. It is not a natural part of the organic vessel.

The higher order fact is, that the human DNA cannot be tampered with without consequences on a collective level. What happens to the DNA in one human can be reproduced in all humans over time due to the interconnected bio-fields, within the joint holographic resonance fields and the racial grids. Tampering with the DNA in one human, will interfere with the archetype of all human DNA. It is just a matter of time before the critical mass is reached. Then what was done for one, becomes the norm. It follows the Law of the One.

Moreover, the human genome is interconnected to other worlds in ways, we are lightyears away from understanding. Humans harm more than doing good in their infantile research and experimentation to regain better health.

Healthy ways of Living – Yes Please
Humans are, generally speaking, far from accepting the common-sense consequences of a wrongful diet, stressful ways of living and all of the other forms of negative energetic influences, which affect our DNA. That includes diseases, we normally think as heritable. This has all been shown in epigenetics, however the implementation of this

into everyday life is still lacking. It is more logical to change the ways, we conduct our lives, how we think, feel and what we eat, than to depend on the long categorizations of DNA editing.

Why mess with the basics and then keep up the ways that create generate unfortunate changes in the human DNA?

Humans are eager to fix things but not so eager to remove the causes, since that demands changes and letting go of ideas and ways of living, most think are important to uphold. However, as many have claimed over the course of history; all diseases are the end-result of wrongful use of energy and consciousness. DNA mutation included along with recessive genes and heritable changes in the genome.

So, why not instead try to understand our reality from the higher order progression ways for our race, what it is made of and ourselves seen in context to this perspective? If we did so, we would enter into an exploration journey of what the higher order sciences might be. If we choose that, we could be able to return to an understanding of what we actually are.

We would move towards a progressive lifestyle, lived from a higher awareness point of view, where we can work with the energy system and the code sheets behind our organic vessel. We can remove the energetic distortions before they turn into illness.

For humanity to reach the apex of any human civilization, humanity has to undergo profound changes in self-perception and learn how to work with all that they are.

The Meaning of I

We also need to address the meaning of I. As a progressive human our quest is not about *who* we are but about *what* we are. Are we a base program clone human, a higher order human, a pillar human or a humanoid from another progressive or regressive system? Either way, we are to develop consciousness, our energy system and utilize our lifeforce to achieve mastery of all reality systems in this universe.

Human progression is about rediscovering what function we had, when we entered this solar system and what we came here to do, or what we came here to learn, utilizing energy and consciousness. Not just learning about the highly advanced technologies our solar system is built upon and the mastery of these mechanical items, but about the use of consciousness to direct our lifeforce into different forms of energy AND technology.

The reason why the question of who we are becomes redundant is that we have been many personalities in our alternate lives within this universe and in the otherverses, and thus it does not matter who we are or what we are, but what we can do.

We have had numerous dissimilar organic vessels and personalities in various realities and as we remember the other-self versions, we have had, we learn to shift between these functionalities. Not just between the personalities and the organic vessels we had on these timelines, but *what we were able to do and the type of genetics we had.* That includes the energetic-organic genetics and the consciousness units. These were integrated into our alternate selves with the purpose of mastering the lifeforce by upgrading the organic vessel and its energy system. Through our accomplishments, we developed the energetic-organic genetics and the consciousness units; all with the purpose of functioning on higher levels of reality. And we do this in this life as well by mastering our organic vessel and by upgrading it to be able to perceive the higher order worlds.

Thus, what matters is to recall what our capacities were, what our technological skills were and what we have learned in this and other realities. It is about rediscovering our talents and in that be able to work with energy and consciousness in the suitable ways. It is about rediscovering our true consciousness to regain the purpose of why we exist and why we are in this system. And with this knowledge, we can upgrade ourselves from the present-day human, we have become, into the higher order and higher awareness human, we can turn into, if we remove what stands in the way, and develop new skills to do so.

The steps towards a high-performance culture
1. We develop the abilities to administer higher awareness.
2. We develop the higher order society that will arise from such a higher awareness, with empathy and understanding.
3. We learn to deal with the other human races and learn how to collaborate with them. Not as students of their societies, but by using our own innate knowledge and understanding of what it means to be a progressive human.
4. We learn to consciously develop our organic vessels, using the exact understanding of energy and lifeforce, and how to develop our higher order genetics in the template and energy system to integrate the density energies into the bio-field. With that we can follow the stages of the NGC without trepidations.

And with that, it is time to look into the new skillsets, we need as well.

Processing Information

Because of the energetic changes coming our way, it is important to learn how to clear, master and work with energy to be able to update our own template and energy systems, along with the competences to rebuild and renew our energy systems.

On top of that, new ways of thinking are needed too, as in how to process information and how to connect the dots to achieve a higher order perspective of our surroundings and the world, we are part of. Thus, the human mind and brain have to develop into new heights as part of our upgrading process. Because how we think affect our mind-field and thus the possibility of building the accurate radiation field.

The ways, we process information today, are counterproductive to the progressive ways of working with energy. Reality and organic energy change continuously, and our brain is in dire need of synapses and cells that are able to adapt, shift and transform according to the incoming energetic information. New skillsets are required to enable us to work correctly with energy, that is from ideas to manifestation.

First on Ideas and Thought Forms
An idea can be called a thought form. Or a thought pattern. A pattern of energy generates a multidimensional form, whether it is entirely energetic or unfolds into manifest matter (matter is a very comprised type of energy) and that form will generate an effect on an individual and on a collective level, since all energy is part of everything there is.

All higher order ideas must have a higher purpose and a function. Otherwise there is no reason to create them. *The purpose has to lead to or give opportunities for progression and benefit the highest good of the many*. If the energy of the thought form is not high enough or it gets distorted, we have to build another pattern. Hence, we have to refine our ideas to ensure they are intricate and detailed enough. We have to sharpen up to keep the ideas in a pristine shape, also after we are done with the creational process. Otherwise they get distorted, as we have seen with the teaching systems where the creator is gone.[100]

Also; thought forms are an energetic equivalent to the clusters of information the synapses respond to, i.e. the same group of neurons that fire, when a certain energy is activated in the brain.

The activation of the synapses can come from internal or external electrochemical sources, that is from the psychological world or from the outside world. Following the activation potential, the brain fires within the correct group of neurons and synapses to extract the new information into understandable images, or existing thought patterns.

Now, when we build patterns of thought, we can use the present-day information and refine what other humans have built, using the human collective field to build their ideas. We can use what they have observed within reality, defined and added to the accepted concepts, i.e. the ideas found in psychology, sciences, religion, etc. However, all lower order concepts are packed with energetic distortions, such as emotional imprints and biased mind-sets. And the ideas are no better than the brain, the ideas came from. This is important to understand because when we work with information, we also work with energy.

If we do use the DE1 sciences, it must be done from a perspective of seeing it as the foundation from which we create the higher order information. DE1 sciences are to be used as a point of reference, and then we continue the building and refining process. We do this, so we can transform the lower order information by working with it.

---

[100] Ideally, we should erase what we have created, when we have no further use of it.

On Contemporary Information

With the understanding of the who, the why and the what is affecting humanity and the manifested reality, we are part of, our awareness must rise to new concepts and understandings. We cannot get sloppy and blindly accept the contemporary concepts that are being created for us by the ancient factions wanting to keep the outer reality status quo.

Most concepts of information in sciences, news, stories, movies etc., are to be viewed as energetic patterns created to enhance and amplify the distortion fields of thought and emotions, i.e. frequency-based brain processes and the subsequent emotional reactions.

The frequency-based energy in the brain follows the buildup of linearly structured information, including abstract visual patterns, and it affects the existing frequency patterns in the brain, i.e. the mind-field, by altering the neurons, the central nervous system, the electric currents and the energetic sequences related to the coding of the DNA to unfold, fire and express the wanted energy patterns keeping humanity in a state of downsized brain capacity.

The emotional amplification of the emotional distortion field, is affected by the wave vibrations (sound) in words, music, added with visual imaginary and colors. All targeted to downscale the energies of the heart field, the periphery nervous system, the glands and the electrochemical energies (hormonal, transmitter and signal used by the cells to communicate) in the energetic environment in the body.

Whatever is created, is fashioned with the aim of filling the cellular energy with distortion instead or the natural higher order energies.

Henceforth, whenever we read something, watch something, listen to something or in any ways are connected to information from others, we must be cognizant of the influence from the code streams behind the words, the concepts, the images etc.

All information is coded energy engineered to target specific types of frequencies, affecting the human brain and glands, with the purpose of altering the human mind, emotions and body into something that can be affected in this or that direction.

Information is Code Streaming

Does false information exist? No. It is not that simple because what is the true information in a reality based upon holographic principles, created energetically for a purpose of progression or the opposite, all depending on what sector that is playing their programs in the outer reality?[101]

It is not a matter of humanity being misled by false information found in news, sciences, religion or personal information, but about what type of encoding that is being created with the type of information at hand and the question whether we, as humans doing the progression journey, want to participate in that form of energy or if we dismiss it, and choose something else; preferably our own higher information stemming from our template.

What is the Beneficial Information?

Beneficial information, as in what we can use to our advantage in our progression work, all depends on the relative reality, we are part of, i.e. the sector we are existing in as in the way we perceive reality via our belief systems and chosen perception of what is good for us and

---

[101] Of course, there exist deliberately false information, created to earn money. And yet again, who is behind these businesses of disinformation, targeting specific groups within humanity to make them believe something?

what is not. It is not a matter of finding the correct information to truly wake up, but to learn to discern between the different forms of energy in the selected information, and choose whether or not we let our brain be coded with the energies of that information. If we let it code our lower order fields, defining the electrochemical milieu in the bio-organic field, or if we clear it out and transform it into its higher order version. It depends on what energy we want to express in this world; that is what we want our fields to hold of energy patterns imprinted into our energy system by the information we have read, seen and integrated from the sources, we have partaken in.

Our fields adapt to these energies and from this, our entire being - from an organic to an energetic level - correspond and express these encoded patterns. We become the beacon of energy for the agenda behind the provided information. Information carries the signature of its creator, and that goes with all information.

Therefore, through the encoded energy in our fields, since energy consists of units within a holographic pattern where all units carry the imprints of the whole, we participate energetically in the sector that gave us the information, the videos, the news, the movies and so forth, we have enjoyed as entertainment or information, teaching us something, or plain downsized information with no use at all, seen from an energetic point of view, other than to generate distortions.

Reality and information about reality are engineered to imprint our energies with the purpose of modifying our energetic sensing of reality from a distorted perspective and not from the higher order perception, we could achieve if we regained our original perception field. If we worked to see things as they truly are, we could get a long way, letting go of the downsized concepts, our world is so full of.

Besides, from the information we have entertained, the segments can, via the holographic principles of co-interaction between unit and wholeness and the feedback mechanism, access our energy fields and from that drain and manipulate our perception field.

Inner Information is Code Streaming
In this, we also have to question the agenda behind the information we receive from inner sources; be it telepathically or via visual aids. The same rules apply here. As long as the information is given from a differentiated source, it will always be part some sort of agenda and the question is if we want to participate in that.

Again, discernment is at play here. Some of it can be useful for us to learn from, and some of it is not. Some of the inner information is manipulated and some is inserted into our mind-field to make us unfold certain features. And also, some of it is actually our own.

And yet again, it is all a matter of discernment and observation of the effects of the received information, whether or not it is amplifying us to unfold more of our genetic content into the human brain, or if it is clogging and creating more distortion. The energetic patterns of the information, in the words and the content, as well as in the visual aid, will give away the purpose and which level of our energy system the patterns are targeting.

Trusting Information?
It is not a matter of trust. Trust is for the ones that have not taken on the responsibility of their own progression journey, and are relying on the information from others. We can use the information from other sources, but we always have to question it, observe the effects of it and how it affects us. Observe the results of the information; does it generate a higher vibrational function and upgrade the brain capacity and in that, sparks us to get more memories and awareness?

As a higher awareness human, we joggle with energy all the time. We participate in a strategic way in our reality setting, knowing that all information is encoded and functions as coding, and that all sorts of energy codes our fields and ultimately the body. And consequently, it is not a question of trusting a source of information, but about if we can use it to develop our genetics and our consciousness capacity. If the code sequences in the information are high enough energetically to activate our genetics in our template or if it is based upon human emotions and human belief systems, which in no case will activate our higher awareness potentials.

We are to
1) Choose what energy we want to express and become part of, and determine if it develops our higher awareness or keeps us in the downsized human brain waves and neural patterns.

2) Choose who and what we want to become by the choices of the coded energies we partake in, expressing the holographic principles of our reality field.

3) Create our own patterns of energy to code our energy system to unfold our potentials. For this we can use the information from others, but be aware of "malware" and distortion codes, which are also a huge part of the information on the internet.

4) Do this until our consciousness genetics begin to unfold their innate knowledge from our true knowledge base, unfolding the higher order sciences, we hold from the manifestations, we have had before this expression of who we are today.

Creating Higher Order Ideas

When we make our own creations and set up our inner and outer life to reconnect all we do, and are, to the higher order standards of the progressive worlds, by the use of the Principles, the Rules and the Laws, we move beyond the collective field of lower order energy. We allow for the possibility of reconnecting to the higher order systemic networks of progression opportunities.

It is important to grasp this, because today most of the human idea-making is part of the collective field of lower order energy and therefore of no use to us, if we want to change the world into a higher order society. The new ideas of the future are not to be found within the DE1 faculties of mind. If they were, they would have been invented ages ago and be part of our world today. And the higher order society, we aim for, is not within any of the contemporary ideas of the future of our planet and its technological achievements.

All the higher order ideas and creations – following the advanced sciences, we once were able to process - have to originate from the higher structural networks in our brain by tapping into the sequenced knowledge stored in our template, and the higher order genetics, to amplify our brain field in a positive and constructive way.

Later on, we will learn to work with energy in its highest order, as code sequences, but before we get to the higher order perception and sight, we must develop our inner seeing and perceiving abilities from viewing energy as pictures or colors, and into energy patterns.

Energy patterns bear a resemblance to manifolds[102] in their 4th to 5th dimensional varieties, although the energy patterns in our fields

---

[102] Manifold https://en.wikipedia.org/wiki/Manifold

are not founded upon mathematical equations. The original energy patterns are composed of the density code sequences of a middle to higher order. The lower order energy patterns are of course made of emotional and mental energies, i.e. of the lowest order sequences.

What the mathematical equations show, if we were to transform the energy patterns into mathematical equations, are code sequences in a lower order variation. In other words; mathematical equations are the human equivalent to the higher order true code systems.

Once we gain the higher order faculties to work with the density holographic arithmetic along with the abilities to see the true code sequences - which mostly resemble rows and rows of transformable signs of an unknown origin – it will be possible to combine the higher order code sequences with the lower order mathematical equations in science. This could change the matter forms of our world into the higher order density energies – as in the ability to work on both levels of the human brain (i.e. using the lower order mind and the higher order consciousness), and from that bridge present-day sciences with the higher order sciences of the future. If that possibility unfolds, all levels of matter could be reconnected to the density energies.

If a large portion of humans were willing to do the required changes for that possibility to unfold, the forced-on systemic resetting of our solar system could potentially be halted. Instead, our system would be recognized as a system that has chosen to work its own way back to the progressive worlds and follow the higher order standards. Such systems are called transition systems.

On an individual scale - for the non-mathematics - the capacity to see and understand energy patterns, as we acknowledge them in our own fields and in our surroundings, will over time lead to the code reading abilities, once our brain capacity is developed to process this type of information.

Consequently, the ability to read and sense energy patterns, as a new way of processing information, is the most optimal method of perceiving energy and an important one, since everything that is built of energy consists of energy patterns. The information of who created the energy patterns, and why they were created, are stored within the energy patterns. Just like all technology holds the imprint of its engineer and the purpose of it. Therefore, reading of energy patterns is the key to unravel how all energetic forms were created.

Contrary to the common ways of processing information, which for most part are just the juggling with introjected information from other human sources as in taught in school or found on the internet and so forth, the ability to read the code sequences directly, as well as seeing the secondary level of all manifested energy as an energy pattern, will give humans the accurate information about their world, of other humans and of their surroundings.

Everything will be out in the open. Nothing will be cloaked in a distortion layer, or any other method to hide the systemic setup of our reality and its true progression purpose. Nothing will have to be taught. All can be read energetically and directly by the observer and in that reading, gaining all the needed information.

The Creational Process

The ability to work with and understand the idea of energy patterns, information sequences and thought forms is important, since it is the best method to create new notions of reality and what the purposes and functions are of that reality, we want to be part of. With the pioneering concepts, and how to build them, we generate our own jurisdiction from which we are in control of every energy unit, we utilize and produce. We define our own reality by doing so.

202

Subsequently, the steps of the creational process become equally important. In the creational processes and idea-making to make any manifested output, such as a product or concepts of thought, we will always begin with what we have available to us. Most of this is part of the lower order concepts and existing ideas. The goal for us is to able to transform the lower order information, we have been taught in this life, into its higher order equivalent. We are to permeate all our lower order information with the higher order consciousness units, stored in our template. The descent happens in a way similar to an osmosis process and we are to clear what stands in the way for that process to happen. We create the possibility for a reconnection to the progression world sciences and standards.

The Principles, the Rules and the Laws assist us in the process of transforming all energy and information. Whatever comes our way, or whatever we create of ideas, we can test it all to see if it fits the requirements of the Principles, the Rules and the Laws. If not, we will let whatever go or create new higher ideas.

As an example; we do not create products to make money alone. That is a natural side effect of good products. The main purpose of all of our creations, products and ideas is that we create to enable our world to reconnect to the progression worlds by lifting its energies in all that is done here. We are the ones to secure that.

Thus, our ideas, creations and products are part of that goal and because of that, our creations, products and ideas are in alignment with the Principles, the Rules and the Laws. Otherwise, whatever we create will just be another case of manifested lower order energy, based upon wrongful utilization of the energies of our reality. And that always lead to more regression in and around us.

Whatever we create will energetically be connected to and part of our energy system. Hence, it is our responsibility to make it perfect.

The Transformation Process

The transformation process of the lower order ideas to their higher order equivalent, is a piece of energy work similar to the work we do, when we clear our fields to allow for the higher order energies to come back in.

In the transformation of the lower order ideas to the higher order ideas and their forms of energy; i.e. energy patterns and information sequences, we are just working with concepts of thought instead of personal memories and similar visual and auditive information. The lower order ideas are to be cleared in the same way.

With these steps of making new systems of thought, from where we perceive and interact with the world in new ways, we prepare for a potential link up to the progressive worlds in the future.

Because, by preparing for that possibility, we take part in creating and manifesting it. The more humans that work for the return to the progressive worlds, the higher order standards and ways of existence, the more likely the possibility of this changes into a probability. And only probabilities manifest.

Besides, if we want to get the benefit of the NGC it goes without saying, that this way, is the way to follow the waves of changes.

New Terminologies

In essence, to fully progress we have to create new terminologies and concepts to be able to explain the pioneering contexts of reality, since none of them currently exist in contemporary systems of thought.

Of course, when we do it this way, it makes it difficult to have a dialogue about the new systems of thought with other humans that do not have the same terminology, but if we do not do it this way, we cannot conceptualize the new ideas of the higher order information.

New ideas need new terminology; otherwise it is just a replication of what is already created and we have to generate a space of energy for the new systems of thought. So, we are to learn a new language and at the same time it will in a way segregate us from the rest of the ideas out there – and other humans too – but it has to be that way for now.

Over time, we will learn to translate the new terminology into similar ideas within the common landscape of thought, if we want to explain it to others. Or we just understand it is like being a rocket scientist and our frames of reference are different than what other people are prefer to know.

However, it does not make us better; it just gives us an expanded version of reality, most people are not willing to look into yet. They prefer the known and we prefer to expand and learn new concepts, which enable us to juggle with the higher and lower order realities of our world.

New Adjustable Paradigms

In the long run, humanity must learn to develop open and responsive paradigms to allow for a continued energization in the brain to match the incoming levels of information, they are to get acquainted with in the future.

Today´s paradigms tend to be closed systems of thought based upon scientific foundations and ideas, generated some 200 years ago and therefore a specific perception of reality. These outdated systems of thought are not allowing for new concepts, or innovative ways of processing information. And pioneering frameworks are required for the progressive energies to blossom within our energy system. We need evolving and adaptable frameworks of reality able to adjust to the constant-in-the-move information systems, which will surface in the future.

The continuously fluctuating information systems, all reality fields are made of, basically consist of holographically imprinted energy units kept together in a holographic grid or soft edged matrix structure.[103]

The energy units and the holographic grids are unfolded within large energy fields. Each field has identical sequences of imprinted energy units but with minor variations to make room for diversity. Otherwise it would be a unity field with little to no possibility for changes.

---

[103] Meaning, the matrix is not squared. Holographic grids are infinite but are defined by the different densities and sub-dimensions, generating a local environment in the overall infinite resonance fields.

Consequently, the reality fields are not rigid and unchangeable. They have only been so due to the stabilizing core crystal pillar grid, which were inserted to level out the uncertain and unstable replication and ripple effects, stemming from the timeline event.

As the NGC alters the resonance fields, holographic and racial grids within the 3-9 pillar activation and cleanup cycle, our magnetic field will change as well. Right now, the magnetic field repels higher order energies, keeping us in the DE1 section of the universe. As the sun shifts its code sequences into DE2 in 2022, our magnetic field will be infused with DE2 radiation and vibration energies instead of the DE1 energies, it has been fueled with so far. This will alter the holographic grids within our energy system and in the reality fields.

In all progressive systems, the reality fields are constructed within the modalities of possibilities and probabilities and the ensuing probable outcome they can unfold within the settings of the larger holographic resonance fields, which lie beneath all manifest realities.

Furthermore, all reality fields regulate their code sequences and energy units to the numerous other reality fields within the group of adjacent systems and universes, a system is part of. And our reality fields will be fine-tuned to the incoming energies from the connected-to-our-system progressive resonance fields, we once were entangled with, fueling the holographic grids of our system along with the sun.

The reality fields are built of radiation and vibration energies. These two forms of energy are part of our energy system as well. Thus, our energy systems correlate to the reality fields, affecting these and are being affected by them too. So, when we create new energy patterns utilizing the lower order fields, be it emotional or mental patterns in our processes of feeling and thinking, we create more distortion and add to the pollution of our reality. In essence, we work against the NGC. Because of this, in our creational processes, we have to utilize the higher order energies in all that we do, and that includes how we think and how we feel. The Principles, the Rules and the Laws are the beginning of this correct formation of energy.

Overview

- All progressive energy units are congregated in holographic grids, composing the holographic resonance fields.
- The holographic resonance fields are the foundation of realities.
- The holographic resonance fields are based upon sequences of information, that express certain possibilities and probabilities.
- Within the holographic resonance fields certain probabilities are unfolded; these are the clusters of information, often connected to a timeline or code stream.
- A timeline is a developed section of the holographic grid, where a sequence of information has generated a probable outcome, i.e. a determined sequence within the holographic resonance field.
- Within such a code stream, or timeline, energy patterns become possible, since they are manifested groupings of energy units.
- All energy patterns then begin to define the probable outcome of the main field, by affecting the remaining possibility rate of that field. The more defined energy patterns a reality field holds, the less opportunity for changes there is.
- A holographic resonance field is completed, when it is composed of sequences of timelines and energy patterns. All energy units, timelines and energy patterns must be according to the highest purity rate, the highest standards and the highest progression rate. If not, that field has to be cleared of the distortions to regain its flexibility. This is called a reset. After this, the field can unfold new possible outcomes.

All of these dynamics and mechanics will become clear as our system regains its original composition, and humanity becomes sensitive to energy again. Although, as long as humans only develop their brains within the frequency-based ways of processing information, it is not possible to work with the progressive information on the higher order levels. Only by expanding the brain's capacity, is it possible to grasp the wholeness of the universal complexity, the many reality fields of sequenced energy and consciousness, the possibility and probability energy units and how the holographic principles truly work.

Therefore, the contemporary reductive and deductive ways of working with information have to change into new ways of thinking, where we work with information as clusters of energy, which can adapt to larger cycles of energy, and not just as part of our local environment.

Information systems of a higher order, are systems that develop and change because reality fields develop and change. And humans are to learn to live in and be part of a changing reality.

To meetup with this changing world, humans are to upgrade, adjust and adapt in a much more efficient way than hitherto. Humans must expand all that they are energetically and consciously. Our world must become a high-performance culture to meetup with the requirements of the future.

The Expanded Human

With the understanding that reality expands inside and outside of us, to higher forms of energy and reality fields, we also understand that – since we exist here – we are far more than just organic matter. Let us recap a bit, before moving on:

The Organic Bio-Field
The organic bio-field fuels our DNA, the molecules and organic vessel, and it bridges - due to its atomic composition – directly into the DE1 quantum fields and because of that, the bio-field is fixed to the older versions of reality energy, until we learn to develop it. Our bio-field is equally influenced by what we eat and ingest, which is why we must change our food habits into only consisting of vital food from natural sources, i.e. a plant-based diet, and not from other lifeforms.

The Emotional Field
Our emotions have their own field, which in its lower order version is called *the emotional field* and in the higher order version is called *the vibrational field* or *the heart field*. The emotional field supports our sensing of the ocean of lower order energies, our world is composed of. The human sensing faculties happens thru the reduced periphery nervous system and the feed-back system into the glands, producing the electrochemical transmitters and signal-givers sent to the brain. From these inputs the brain processes the energetic information.

Aside from the downsizing of the overall energetic sensitivity due to wrongful diet and lack of practice, whatever we sense and perceive depends on what we allow to ourselves to transform into cognizant understanding. The interpretation mechanism of the brain is limited by our cognitive capacity and personal narrative of what a human can and is. However, if we adjust our self-perception and our narrative of what we are, along with clearing the emotional field from energetic clutter and the self-created limiting energy patterns, we can develop and transform the emotional field into the vibrational field. With the higher energies running in our emotional field, the periphery nervous system unfolds new sensing faculties. As soon as the vibrational field functions as it is supposed to, it connects to the chiasm and expands the periphery nervous system into its higher order version. Following that achievement, we are able to sense the different forms of energy our reality is truly made of from the frequency-based energies to the higher order energies in the multiple realities linked to our system.

Our comfort zone determines how much we are willing to sense and perceive. We are the primary adversary of our higher order faculties because of our innate fears. Fear of the unknown and of death are the two strongest limitations to expanded awareness.

The Mental Field
Our mental field governs the brain processes and it is limited to only being able to process the electromagnetic input from the lower order bio-field and the distorted emotional field. Thus, we need to clear the mental field of old belief systems and downsizing systems of thought.

In its higher order version, the mental field is called *the brain field* and it is part of *the multi-density radiation field* that detects, discerns, and assimilate the energetic information from the surroundings as well as processing the timeline energetic information from the heart field. The brain is thus far more than just a set of neurons thrown into different areas of the brain; it is a complete and profound network of pathways beginning with the lower order neuro-synaptic pathways, ranging into the higher order structural layers composed of density energy, matching the reality fields the brain field is connected to.

To be able to use the brain field capacity, the functionality of the brain has to be developed. It has to become accustomed to process information via the expanded perception field, the brain is capable of producing, once the heart field is operating correctly. The incoming higher order energies from the chiasm and into the vibrational field, fuel the brain field and in that, send the needed energy to the brain, from where it can expand its field into other realities.

From that expanded perception of reality and what we learn from the vibrational and radiation fields, generating the correct energy, we can develop into being able to use the comprehensive consciousness structure, we have stored in the template and begin the descent of this into the higher order structural layers of the brain. The higher order cognitive faculties can be utilized to perceive the otherverses and the other-dimensional systems outside the known and accepted reality. From that, we understand that our present-day perception of what a human is, is too narrow and that we can expand to become so much more. We begin to hold higher order sciences and possibilities.

We choose to progress, in this bio-organic vessel, to be capable of perceiving the true version of our world and the other worlds, and in that learn to master energy and consciousness in this reality and the other realities. However, to do this, we must be ready to change our personal narrative of what we are and what we are capable of.

The Correct Ways
The correct ways of perceiving and being aware, for humans in our reality, follows the higher order progressive energies. Our goalsetting and daily utilization of energy have to change from the mindless and blindfolded use of the energies into a conscious progression of reality

for the betterment of all, where all that we do are seen in the light of progressing our energy system as the first challenge, to allow for the higher order conscious units to descend into the bio-organic vessel. The true way we were supposed to exist.

Thus, our everyday life must focus on the correct choice-making, using the Principles, the Rules and the Laws to determine what the higher order choices are in what is shown and energetically reflected to us. What is reflected to us are within the occurring circumstances, people, in the line of events etc., as we move from the morning time into the evening time, utilizing the different energies of the day. Our choice-making will regulate what type of energy we circulate in our three lower fields and into our energy system, since the higher order energy system can only bridge into the bio-field, if the emotional and mental fields are upgraded to their higher order version.

The mastery of energy is not just about how to achieve all the correct solutions to rebuild our three lower fields with progression energies, but also the contemplative progression work with whatever is stored in our higher order energy system to develop, rebuild and remaster what we are on all levels of our current, past and future existence.

Through the choices we do, according to the challenges at hand, we act consciously within the frame work of reality energy and from that enable the Principles, the Rules of Engagement and the Natural Laws of Energy Utilization to work in our favor.

In other words, by accomplishing the correct choices in whatever is presented to us on an everyday basis, the energy from the correct choices will push us upwards in the progression spiral, or downwards into the regression spiral, if we go against the progression energies of our system. The lesser optimal choices, leading to regression, are the choices that urge us to go against the progression energies.

The lesser order choices are found within the lower order human matrix of limited belief systems and emotional resistance, because of fears of change and the unknown. The comfort-zone keep most stuck in the lower order energies of our reality.

Every choice, be it a thought, an emotional response, an action or a decision determine what type of energy, we utilize and in that, what the outcome of the daily sequence of possible progression will be. This observance is how we develop our three lower fields into their higher order version in the progressive energy system. Because, what we are energetically, will be mirrored to us from the outside and from the inside, so we can figure out and learn how to rebuild along with remastering what we once were and from that, change what we can become.

The transition work of the day should be to progress all lower order challenges to their higher order possibilities, as well as to transform whatever is presented to us into a possible choice of progression.[104]

The chiasm, and the timeline work, must also be used in the rebuilding of an energy system able to implement the higher order energies. In this work, it is important to understand that every density field, and its sub-dimensions, has its own organization of reality. We need the correct coding in our energy system to work within that field. We only have that, if we have done it before as part of the pillar projects.

The ability to use *the higher order senses* comes back when the heart field, the brain field, and the central and periphery nervous systems as well as the cells, reactivate and are able to carry the higher order energies. Which brings us to the next chapter.

---

[104] The energetic sequences of the day, month and year are explained in the HAL Advanced Class 2. The system of the daily sequence is called the Rotundum.

Developing Our Higher Order Senses

The understanding of developing who and what we are, by the use of the Principles, the Rules and Laws, is called higher order progression. And new levels of our inner work are to be embraced to progress any further. The work to regain the higher order senses must be done by the individual as a willed choice. It is not something that occurs in all humans, once the original systemic construction becomes part of our reality again. It is this way, because the higher order faculties must be reached for and trained to become part of the current organic vessel.

The higher order senses follow the higher order energies, just like our lower order senses were developed to work with electromagnetic energies. We can work with all versions of energy, low and high, if we develop and practice the higher order senses to detect, process and understand them.

The higher order senses are:
1) the higher order sight or inner sight,
2) the higher order hearing or inner hearing,
3) the higher order tasting,
4) the higher order smelling,
5) the higher order tactile sensing.

The higher order senses are the higher order energy expression of the human senses. They are used within the higher order realities, when we expand our perception field into the other-dimensional levels of our reality. Here they provide higher order perception and information processing on the different segments of the dimensions.

The higher order senses are utilized in the same way as our human sensing faculties. We see something or hear something on the inner planes of existence, aka the higher order realities.

The higher order seeing occurs through the mind's eye, similar to when we get visions or have dreams. The timeline work consists of visual information, mostly from existences on diverse timelines.

The visual cortex is the one that gets amplified energetically when we have visions, dreams or do the timeline work, and not the eyes. Therefore, part of our clearing work should focus on that area of the brain to enable it to process the higher order energies.[105]

If we have an encounter, it is both the eyes and the visual cortex that are in play, although the encounter is not within our reality, but in the 4D or 5D. As we learn to work with the higher order energies, our eyes develop new abilities and then much more of our reality can be seen, as it appears in another dimensional forms of energy.[106]

The higher order inner hearing is mostly telepathic in nature, or it can be a vocal replay from a memory, or a timeline sequence.

The inner hearing is not identical with the outer hearing. When the humanoids talk to us – not telepathically because that is mostly sent as images and energetic information – but in vocal (speaking English or their native language) it is felt in the auditory cortex of the brain[107] more than heard with the ears. It is so, for the reason that they talk within our sphere of reality and not from the outside. The sounds are energetic and thus only our auditory cortex is amplified.

The higher order seeing and hearing dependent on a developed brain field, since both utilize the perception field as the transmitter of energy from the other dimensions and into our physical brain, where the energies are transformed into information.

---

[105] https://en.wikipedia.org/wiki/Visual_cortex
[106] The typical clairvoyance is mostly visual information from the distortion planes.
[107] https://en.wikipedia.org/wiki/Auditory_cortex

As we grow accustomed to sense within and the other realities being part of our perception field, we develop the faculties of tactile sensing, smell and taste. The higher order tactile sensing occurs as we sense the other-dimensional fields, entities and humanoids entering into *our expanded sphere of reality*. Our body will respond to their occurrence as if they were physically present, which they technically are, but in the 4D or 5D.

Higher order smell is interesting, because quite a lot of the 4Ds have a distinct scent to their organic forms. That other-dimensional scent will be there if and when they choose to enter into our sphere of reality. Similarly, to when humans emit scents from their vessel.

Higher order taste is fascinating as well, given that some of the regressed emit a sort of energy that gives a bad taste in the mouth or cause nausea, as if we have eaten something disgusting.

Scent, sound and organic presence are waveforms of energy, being emitted from any organic vessel. Therefore, we can sense the other-dimensional races just as we sense other humans within our realm of reality. We do not just see or hear other humans; subconsciously we sense the energy of others via the nervous system and the sensitivity of the skin. It is just our brain and our sensing abilities that need an upgrade to be able to function correctly on the subtle levels of our expanded reality.

The higher order sensing, smell and taste are used to determine what is occurring within our expanded sphere of reality. As it is with the experiences of disgusting smell, taste and nauseating sensing of other humans, it is correspondingly with whatever decides to appear to us from the other realities. What feels bad is bad. But what feels good, is not necessarily good, due to the holographic cloaking technologies.

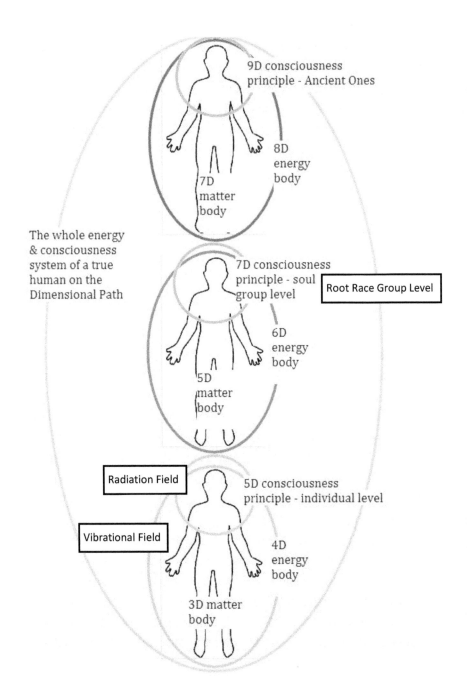

9D consciousness
principle - Ancient Ones

8D
energy
body

7D
matter
body

The whole energy
& consciousness
system of a true
human on the
Dimensional Path

7D consciousness
principle - soul
group level

Root Race Group Level

6D
energy
body

5D
matter
body

Radiation Field

5D consciousness
principle - individual level

Vibrational Field

4D
energy
body

3D matter
body

Energy, Consciousness and Life

All there is, fundamentally speaking, is energy, consciousness and life. Nothing else. All universes are composed of these three components. Components that can be altered into smaller units, as for example the template codes, or stretched into a larger complex pattern composing an organic lifeform, a reality or a solar system.

Understanding the Resonance Fields
All progression realities are organic and energetic in construction and are composed of density units (radiation), density energies (vibration) and density fields. All lifeforms are an expression of the radiation and vibration energies, and they all partake in developing the large energy fields providing the foundation of realities; i.e. the resonance fields. The resonance fields *reverberate* with the vibration energies, creating the timelines, the organic vessels and the heart field in every lifeform, whereas the radiation energies *amplify* the holographic grids and the racial networks, along with the brain field and its consciousness units.

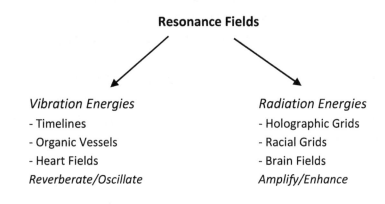

Resonance Fields

Vibration Energies
- Timelines
- Organic Vessels
- Heart Fields
Reverberate/Oscillate

Radiation Energies
- Holographic Grids
- Racial Grids
- Brain Fields
Amplify/Enhance

All progressive human energy systems and their realities are built of combinations of these forms of energy. Resonance fields are ruled by *energetic and genetic affinity*, which means that all density energies vibrate, radiate and resonate with everything that is similar to them. These dynamics create *order, balance and harmony*. Everything that is dissimilar, is repelled or evaporated.

If the vibration energy cannot be aligned with an alien energy source, be it from a human or a reality, it repels the alien energy source. The radiation energy responds in a similar manner. If the radiation energy cannot amplify the interfering energy, it evaporates the source of it. Hence, vibration energy repels and radiation energy evaporates in the protective version and in the peaceful version the energies align and amplify (which is the true understanding of Principle 2).

This means that the progressive worlds cannot connect to us until we have transformed our energy systems to contain progressive energies. Otherwise any encounter is repelled or even worse, our consciousness units evaporate. Equally, we cannot connect to the progressive worlds either, hence the building of the rehabilitation zones.

Numerous attempts have been made to send in adapted progressive humans, but all failed due to the reversed laws and dynamics, which the mission humans were forced to operate under, once they entered.

The NGC will not be influenced by these regressed dynamics, since it runs from the core facilities in all constructions, and not by humans. This also means, that we need progressed humans within our reality to ground the NGC, and to align its energies within our reality fields. And yet again, these humans need to be fully aware of what is to be preserved and what needs to go, to enable our system to follow the progressive purity rates, standards and progression rates.

Chaos as the Beginning and the End

Progressive realities unfold from states of lesser to higher density, i.e. from a less developed system into a highly ordered system, meaning that lesser developed systems contain few progressed consciousness units with a high degree of raw or, in the end, of outdated energy.

All cycles begin in *a productive chaotic state*, full of potentials and possibilities with lots of raw undefined energy, and all cycles run out in *a state of unproductive chaos* with outdated and depleted energy with no potentials or possibilities.

In the middle, between the states of productive and unproductive chaos, the highly ordered systems exist. They are built of transformed energy and hold a high degree of developed consciousness units.

The Density Worlds

In the new worlds there are less order, balance and harmony due to a low degree of conscious building and the Principles, the Rules and the Laws are not integrated yet. New worlds are raw and undefined, and they hold a *higher possibility rate* and a *lower probability rate*. Every outcome is uncertain. The timelines are undefined.

In comparison, higher order worlds are made of large amounts of consciousness units and the reality energies have been transformed into constructions, technologies and creational projects by the use of consciousness. Therefore, the higher order worlds hold a high degree of order, balance and harmony, and all outcomes are easily predicted because of *a higher probability rate* and *a lower possibility rate*. Most of the timelines have been defined and there is less uncertainty, since the new timelines most likely will be similar to the existing ones.

In the higher order worlds, all energy fields and units are infused with consciousness units and consequently, a higher order world is a multifaceted world with enormous amounts of complex information systems and developed resonance fields exemplifying a lot of coding, where all the consciousness and energy units have been altered into a creational expression by the humans living there.

Similarly, a progressive human in a higher order world has a high degree of advanced consciousness units integrated into the template. The energy system has been developed over many lifetimes and it is composed of transformed energy, modified several times by the code sequences built into it to fit different purposes and functions.

Humans from the higher order worlds emit a multifaceted kind of radiation and vibration energies, due to their advanced configuration, consisting of accumulated experiences, knowledge and proficiency. Unsurprisingly, a human from a lesser developed world is undefined and energetically raw with an uncomplicated consciousness structure and an energy system with little information built into it.

In essence, the higher order worlds are made of consciousness units interplaying with the holographic radiation units, vibration energies and the resonance fields. All realities and humans are progressed by the many consciousness-holographic developmental programs, upheld by the encoded holographic grids.

These worlds are administered by state-of-the-art technologies; all of which are beyond contemporary human comprehension. All lifeforms are engineered from multifaceted code systems, i.e. the template and the energy system. Both are needed to unfold an organic vessel.

All density forms, creations, technologies and realities can be read by the observer, since whatever is built, is built of code sequences made by energy and consciousness. Every single energy unit, as well as the consciousness units, are holographic. This means that each unit holds the entire coding of what it is part of, or have been part of. Each unit is an access point into the whole, from which is has been taken.

All energy units reverberate or get amplified, when they interact with progressive consciousness. The reverberation dynamics are utilized in horizontal development programs, where the lot of the many defines their plane of existence. The amplification dynamics are used when the plane of existence is to be upgraded.

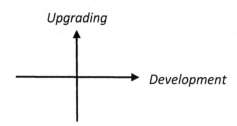

All technologies are administered by the engineer, using advanced holographic creational and developmental programs. Also, if further technologies are to continue the initial programs, when the engineer is gone. Everything that is made holds the consciousness signature of its engineer and nothing can be left behind anonymously. When the engineer moves on, everything has must be erased. Otherwise the engineer is linked to his or her creations. Unless, of course, what is left behind serves a general purpose for continued expressions of life, similar to the structures and constructions made by the Ancient Ones.

This information is vital in our template and timeline work. Whatever, we might encounter, holds inbuilt information systems, from which we can get how it is built, what it is made of and how to dissimilate or amplify it in our clearing work.

When we have built in enough progressive energies into our energy system, we can use the laws of energetic and genetic affinity to clear out what is unwarranted in our expanded sphere of reality, as well as in our timeline clearing work.

On Order, Balance and Harmony

The progressive worlds expand and grow within what can be termed *unity consciousness* and it is the progressive consciousness structure for both genders. If we were to liken it with something, we can relate to, it would be a sort of female consciousness structure.

The unity consciousness rests upon order, balance and harmony within organizations of progression. It works to achieve the highest good for all. It is a social and community-based observance of reality.

The unity consciousness is not about being aligned with the group and having no individual say in anything, but about living in concord with the notion of protecting the joint reality fields and all that lives there.

It is focused on developing all reality fields through the understanding of what is the highest good for all, and by that, enable all root races to progress according to the energies of the grand cycles.

All the root races progress as a unity of races within connected reality fields, and there is no need for warring, competition or them-against-us mentality.

Correspondingly, the male consciousness structure came to be when the humanoid races arose as an opposition to the progressive worlds. The *humanoid consciousness* rests upon the dynamics of diversity and advantage, within organizations of trade and competition to the brink of warring. It works entirely to achieve individual goals, even to the negative cost of others, and it is a self-centered observance of reality.

The Humanoid Consciousness

It has become evident over the course of events, that the attempts to seed in the humanoid consciousness into all realities, along with their bending and alteration of the Principles, the Rules and the Laws, have led to nothing but disaster for all involved races.

The humanoid consciousness has led to a brutal seeking of power over others, in the attempts to gain knowledge and mastery of energy without any consideration for the whole or the individuals, they have been praying on to maintain their own existence.

The humanoid consciousness structure is solely working for the maximum gain of the individual and what is considered the greatest good for one race, and not for the other races. The diversity thinking has led the humanoids to consider themselves superior.

And lastly, the humanoid consciousness has brought nothing but disruptive chaos, perversion of worlds that should be righteous and just, along with the distortion and the formation of death, as well as the rise of illness.[108]

In that, it must be conceived that the humanoid consciousness has not lived up to its function to develop consciousness units within the grand cycles and their energies, and that it must be upgraded to serve any further purpose.

With that in mind – and considering that humanity is fixed into the humanoid consciousness structure and they live accordingly on an everyday basis – the big challenge for humanity, and the otherverses observing the humanoid consciousness, is the transition into the unity consciousness structure, within the progression cycles and according to the incoming energies of the NGC.

---

[108] Death and illness are not a natural. Both occur due to wrongful use of energy and consciousness.

225

The Natural Order

Contrary to the regressed humanoid worlds, the progressive realities work within the unity consciousness constructions, where life is lived to attain what is considered to be the highest good of the many.

Naturally what that is, is decided within the councils and the joint assemblies of all realities. This decision-making generates a peaceful co-existence in the progressive worlds.

Moreover, as a consequence of the Principles, the Rules and the Laws, a natural order arises. It is so, because all progressive humans strive to accomplish and create what benefits the individual human, the root races and the joint fields of existence.

Progressive humans know that the goal of working with energy is to achieve the highest purity rate, the highest standards and the highest progression rate. Why? To ensure the highest possibilities for all races living in the joint fields of existence. If all work for this, the realities are kept in a pristine shape, providing the best circumstances for all.

The progressive humans do not develop merely as individuals but also as a team, because the progressive humans work for the highest good of the many and for the highest progression rate for all.

And not to forget, all progressive humans are strong and competent individuals, all working by their own accord to achieve their goals. And this determined independency is exactly why the Principles, the Rules and the Laws were developed.

Hence, the unity consciousness leads to the accurate self-observance, self-progression and self-responsibility. It is so for the reason that the natural order ensures the accurate position within the developmental programs. If the lesser choices are preferred, the purity rate will drop, the standards of the heart field get lowered and the progression rate gets lowered too.

Consequently, the progressive humans are trialed by their creations, actions and choices. The progression rate that follows this, determines the overall position within the programs and the progression spiral.

Since all progressive humans know this, there are no good excuses for not observing the natural order of things. It is a willed choice to stay within the developmental programs of the progressive realities, or to fall behind. It is a conscious choice, since it is only possible to violate the natural order, i.e. to bend, to break or let go of the Principles, the Rules and the Laws as an active choice with active deeds. As always – there are no victims, there are only stupid choices.

The Natural Balance
Progressive humans will do whatever it takes to observe the natural order and to do what it takes to move up the progression spiral. Due to this, they also acknowledge that the quality of their creations, of their organic vessels and of the reality, they are part of, have to be of the highest degree of excellence.

They want to create the best technologies available. They want to reach the highest vibration in the heart field and bring about the best thinkable timelines, and they want to process the highest version of radiation energy to attain the most expanded brain field to perceive and interact with as many realities as possible.

This is the self-driven competition of any progressive human. The humans of the higher order worlds do not compete with others, but with themselves to perform better, be better and achieve more, since they want to rise to the occasion and given the mere fact that higher order humans are driven by dignity, honor and will.

It follows the logic that the more a progressive human knows, the better he or she can observe the Principles, the Rules and the Laws, and the better he or she will be at building and constructing realities in the most honorable and impeccable manner. Correspondingly, only the highest functional consciousness units and their purified energies, will be transferred into the next cycle.

It should also be clear that a progressive human is a modest person, because only by observing the Principles, the Rules and the Laws will it lead to the complete knowledge and understanding of all worlds. And only the ones having this discipline, will move into the next cycles. The natural balance of existence unfolds from this.

The purpose of life is to progress energy and consciousness into their highest versions, nothing else. All progressive humans live to ensure the cyclical continuation of all energy and consciousness units, along with reaching the highest progression rate in all units.

And finally, progressive humans live to engineer advanced worlds, not by technology alone – that is only a tool – but in the light of the knowledge, understanding and comprehension of each grand cycle.

The Natural Harmony
The last piece follows naturally. Once the natural order and natural balance are acknowledged and accepted as the best imaginable ways to reach the overall purpose of life, natural harmony comes into play. Nobody is unhappy in the progressive realities, since everyone knows their rightful position and function. All progressive humans know that by developing their energy and consciousness units, they can move into a new level of reality, if they choose to do so.

They also know, that they – by their own effort – can fall behind, if they choose to not observe the Principles, the Rules and the Laws.

The progressive realities are fair due to this self-observance and self-responsibility, since any choice, action and deed are done from a level of complete understanding of the consequences.

The HTS

To ensure that understanding of the consequences, the holographic teaching systems (the HTS) became part of the progressive worlds.

The interactive consciousness programs were developed to assist all versions of the developmental programs and to accommodate for the appropriate use of energy by mirroring the content of the energy system. This mirroring was done by unfolding what was in the energy system into holographic scenarios, by the use of the perception field. In the holographic interactive simulations, the consequences of each choice, deed and action would be presented and afterwards it would be up to individual to choose the best option and timeline.

Conclusively, the technologies, the communities and the councils in the progressive worlds are designed to support the highest purity rate, the highest standards and the highest progression rate, and how to get there. Again, progressive humans will naturally choose the most optimal options, from which they want to follow through in order to attain the utmost opportunities for their existence.

The Purpose and Function

As already explained, the first step of the progressive programs was to learn to work with energy and consciousness in an organic vessel and within a lineage, as part of a community. When that was learned, pillar humans would be positioned within various programs, learning how to progress their template, their energy system and their reality by becoming the developers of these 3 levels within various teams, focused on the work of progressing energy and consciousness.

Then the next step would be to become part of the leader teams, administering the progression on a systemic level, i.e. a workstation, with the goal of developing the lineages and root races of that system into their highest purity rate, the highest standards and the highest progression rate for each root race and lineage.

After this, the pillar humans would participate in the holographic-technological levels to advance the energies of the constructions, also into the highest technological purity rate, the highest standards and the highest progression rate for each construction.

Finally, they would learn how to administer a universe along with a group of progressive humans, having mastered how to administer and develop universal energies, into the highest universal purity rate, the highest standards and the highest progression rate for universes, and all of the races existing there.

The main purpose was to learn to administer and progress energy on the reality and systemic levels:

1) Grid energies to their highest purity rate using the Laws.
2) Code streams and timelines into the highest potential futures using the highest standards, i.e. the Principles and the Rules.
3) Developing the highest possible base of knowledge to be able to administer a vast expansion field present in all realities.
4) Unfolding this knowledge into creational projects by the use of code sequences, templates, programs, technologies etc. to further the advancement and optimal use of the reality field potentials into the highest progression rate for all.
5) Excluding the usage of entirely technological driven realities, since the highest progression rate is measured as the quality of the developed energy and consciousness units and not by the technological achievements alone.

The reality and systemic worlds were composed of 5 purposes:

- The ground crew situated in the outposts. Their purpose was to progress and organize the organic forms by the correct use of the racial grids and holographic energy units.
- The developers of the possibilities to progress the timelines. Their purpose was to transform, advance and organize the reality vibrational units to produce suitable energy currents and flows of manifestation.
- The organizers of knowledge and how to obtain knowledge. Their purpose was to transform, advance and organize the reality radiation units to produce suitable fields and worlds.
- The code writers and template builders. Their purpose was to develop and organize the code sheets by the correct use of all energy units along with engineering developmental programs and assisting technologies.
- The councils and the assemblies within the root races. Their purpose was to administer, organize, oversee and process the reality fields, into which these root races unfold.

These functions led to order, balance and harmony in the progressive worlds, because everyone knew their purpose. No one had the need to take away the progression possibilities from their fellow humans.

Progressive humans know this and all observe this. It is a natural way of existing. Within unity consciousness, all works for a common goal, which is strived for. Everybody works towards the same goals of the highest purity rate, the highest standards and the highest progression rate, in spite of the variation within the root races. Every progressive human is unique and that individual uniqueness is unfolded to its highest progression rate. Not as part of diversity and competition but within the understanding of the individual purposes and functions.

In our present-day reality, we can choose to work with energy to clear the individual and collective distortions; not just for ourselves but for the betterment of all. Because the more that get a higher purity rate, the purer the physical energies become and with that, a lesser degree of distortion will be found in the collective fields of our reality.

By observing the Principles, the Rules and the Laws, we assure that we are capable of generating the best possible standards and the highest progression rate for our current world. By implementing these into our lives, we generate a joint field that can follow the original ways of the progressive realities and in that, strengthening the chance for us to generate a bridge to the progressive worlds.

Why Does Failure Exist?
Due to the absence of will, honor and dignity, and because of the pre-dispositions in the consciousness units, not being strong enough to follow through. These pre-dispositions arose from the consciousness structure of the previous cycles, because of the infinite circulation of energy and consciousness expressed into various lifeforms.

And pralaya, or the long rest until the correct cycle for that type of energy and consciousness arises again, is the main cause of failure, the root of the infection and the pre-dispositions leading to a weak will, no dignity and no honor, i.e. the infection of the consciousness units and the contamination of the energy units.

After the NGC, there will be no options for pralaya. This was only an option within the first cycles, where the risk of failure was high.

Besides, as each cycle reaches its final stages, the humans left will understand how to upgrade, how to clear and how to adjust all that could lead to a lesser position within the ensuing cycle. The NGC will ensure that the overall purpose of the human evolution gets back on track. But only for the ones that can and are willing to follow through.

On the Progression Rate

Originally, the pillar human energy system and the progression spiral was working together to develop the progression rate. Therefore, to be able to do the transition work towards a higher order existence, we must learn to administer our progression rate again, in order to be connected to the progression spiral.

The progression rate sets the probabilities of our progression and if we have the needed energy and consciousness units to integrate our higher order awareness into our current organic vessel.

The progression rate also determines the surplus of energies in our energy system, needed to achieve any progressive goals and how quickly they can manifest into our segment of reality.

The quantity of progressive energies in our energy system and the quality of the consciousness units in our template, are reflected in the progression rate as well. Also, if the rate is regressive. Hence, the energetic quantity and the consciousness quality determine how fast we can remove the prohibiting technologies and how quickly we are able to rebuild our template and energy system.

The Manifestation Rate
Therefore, the progression rate determines how quickly we can and are able to manifest changes, but it also determines to what degree we are able to access our higher order knowledge. On the other hand, a higher degree of inner knowledge does not necessarily mean higher manifestation abilities, because this depends on the reality zone, we live in and the level of awareness we perceive reality from.

For humans being part of the extinction zone, it is not possible to manifest in the degree that is looked for. The work in the extinction zone is about clearing and learning about the timelines, choices and purposes of the past. Thus, the main energy work in the extinction zone is to clear all personal timelines part of long-gone worlds to get free of the extinction protocol. It is not about an attempt to rebuild the world, as long as the template structure is outdated and stuck in the past, which is the case for most humans. So, being in the decay zone, also means not really being able to manifest changes.

Similarly, when positioned within the regressed zone, the work is to do the freeing work from the racial contracts and all that follows from this work. It is not to build a new world, before being clear of the regressed timelines and the regressed influences.

And of course, the work within the present-day DE1 areas is to do the transition work from the DE1 and into the DE2, which at first most likely will begin with the downward fall into the extinction zone and then followed by the freeing work within the regressed zone.

The Progression Rate Energy Work

The first step is to transform the old energies of the energy system and template, doing the clearing work, and then move into the new understanding, where the information unfolds naturally from within.

The intuitive knowledge of how to work with the correct energies of our reality, will grow from the work and the level we have gotten to, i.e. what was developed within the original pillar project. We can only work with what we can perceive and hold as inner knowledge.

The progression rate energy work, we do, should be viewed from 4 approaches; the goal we set for our energy work, the time it takes and what can be changed from possibilities into probabilities, along with the changes we want to manifest.

What arises from the 4 approaches will be reflected into our lives, due to the projection mechanism of our energy system and *the innate interaction potentials*, we hold in our template.

234

The developed consciousness units in the template and the level it had reached, set the interaction potentials we have at our disposal.

Hence, whatever our template contains of progressive consciousness units, regressive consciousness units, and lower and higher distortion energies will be reflected into our perception field, and that content will be the context from which we can create new circumstances, new choices and new awareness.

The Principles, the Rules and the Laws are challenged according to the content of our consciousness units and our interaction potentials.

The new choices we are to take to make things right, arise from the interaction potentials played out within events and people, mirroring back to us what we need to work with.

Thus, the best way to activate the innate interaction potentials, with the highest probability for manifested changes, is to work with and follow the Principles, the Rules and the Laws in all that we do. Plus, the more we use these, the more progressive our energy system becomes, and the faster the progression rate generate what we need of knowledge and transformed energy to build our relative reality and our personal chosen progression work.

Finally, the denser the energy units are in our energy system and surroundings, the slower the manifestation rate will be. The clearer our energy system and template are, the easier it will be to manifest in a shorter period of time and the more we will be able to clear the old dynamics of our template, keeping us back.

And not to forget; our goals will manifest according to the reality zone we are part of and the counterforces, finding our goals to be of service to them or the opposite and if so delaying us, along with the question of racial contracts to be released from.

The Breakthrough Point

Once we master our progression rate and are able to optimize our energy, and recreate the code sequences, we become able to push through the point, where we regain the control of our inner and outer reality.

The breakthrough point is the critical mass of energy in our energy system and as long as we are below this, the counterforces can mess with us.

Either way; we are to transform our energy system and whatever, we encounter, will mirror to us what we need to learn to be in concord with the Principles, the Rules and the Laws.

> *So, let us finish off with the Principles, the Rules and the Laws.*
> *They have been updated to bring new energy to their purpose.*

What is a Principle, Rule or a Law?

A Principle, a Rule or a Law are energetic features that define how the energies of a resonance field, the radiation field and the vibrational field will react to an interaction with consciousness units in an organic structure aka a lifeform, along with the reciprocity of these energies.

If the consciousness units are of this or that variety, then that specific level of reality will respond in this or that way, according to the type of consciousness units in that organic vessel. Therefore, the quality of the consciousness units determines how the Principles, the Rules and the Laws unfold energetically when a certain action, thought or deed are activated in that specific field.

With this understanding, not two individuals are under the identical energetic dynamics or the ways the Principles, the Rules and the Laws will be expressed in our lives, unless they stem from the same genetic composition, which is rare (even clones differ in composition). In this it is applied that the laws of energetic interaction for one individual is dissimilar from the laws of another, all depending on the complexity of the template and the energy system, and what have been obtained within various systems and schemes.

The individual quirks and particulars will surface in the work with the Principles, the Rules and the Laws, and the nuances of how to work with energy following these. What is shown and how we respond will define the results and from that, through observation, the individual progression rate and innate abilities can be detected and determined.

On the 12 Principles of Progression

The Principles are the building blocks that enable us to build a higher awareness structure. The Principles, and the way they work in each individual, are based upon the original skills to be re-developed in the attempt to reboot our energy system, so we yet again can follow the original guidelines of the progressive systems.

1. *Only Behave, as We Want Others to Behave*
    This Principle leads to a higher self-responsibility energetically, mentally, emotionally along with a higher order observance in speech, behavior and emotional response to all which are "put in front of us." We behave, as we want others to behave. We act as the role models for what we want in the world.

    Principle 1 is also called the Law of the One; i.e. if one can do it, others can too. Thus, everything we do allow for others to do it as well. So, we better sharpen up.

2. *Respond with Equal Energy and Consciousness*
    The Principle gives the answer of how to interact with humans, not doing the progression work. We respond to their level of awareness and only give them, what they can hold of energy. If we give them more information and energy than they can hold, the chances are high of activating levels in them, which they are not ready to deal with. And in doing so, the feedback to our energy system will be that we are not ready either to hold that awareness, because we cannot administer it yet.

The Principle also allows for actions that can be looked-for in our encounters with the other-dimensionals. Moreover, it sets the standard for dealings with humans, used as a tool to harm us.

However, the use of Principle 2 to defend and to protect is only for activated humans knowing how to work with genetics and energies, aiming at a result for the highest good of the many. The response is not an emission of energy, but the appropriate level of evaporation, and only when we are interfered with.

3. *Only Focus on What We Want to Amplify*
    This Principle is also called *the Law of Participation.* What we focus on, look at, perceive, join, read, watch etc., we connect to energetically and then we participate in the relative reality behind that information. This changes our energetic settings, the code layers and the template, and it allows for a use of our energies to amplify regressed realities and their thought forms within this world. And the progressives, naturally.

    Aside from the effect of our interest on our energy system, we also amplify what we look at. This means, whatever we do not want to exist, we do not amplify by having an interest in it, or by looking at it. We focus on what we want to grow, and what we do not want to exist, we clear and evaporate.

4. *The Outcomes Correspond to What We Are*
    This Principle shows us the inner and outer outcomes of the energies we hold. Not just the energies in this life but from all lives, along with the timelines where we have organic vessels, clones or genetics, and what these engage in energetic. These

239

other versions affect the quality of all energies we hold, pulling them down or uplifting them. The energies are of a higher or a lower standard, depending on the realities they interconnect with. Whatever we hold, runs across all timelines, allowing us to perceive and work with the past, the present and futures of what we are and thus what needs to be changed, cleared and evaporated. Reality and events are the mirrors of what we are.

5. *Inner Knowledge is the Correct Teacher*
This Principle pulls in the information stored in the code sheets and the energy fields in our template. The quality and quantity of the information depends on what pillar template structure we have and the developmental programs we have been part of. That will energetically determine our inner knowledge and what we attain from within. All content has to be investigated and looked upon with the goal of becoming the best version of what we can be, and what needs to be done to get there. Not all we hold are for the highest good of the many.

6. *The Correct Partnerships Will Come Our Way*
This Principle works on the dynamics of either the progression or the regression spiral to attract the appropriate partnerships for us, be it in our clearing work, freeing work or progression work. Partnerships can be any lifeform here or beyond, and we are to work with all of them to either clear out the regressed timelines, we are participating on together, or to build a new reality in the progression work. The appropriate partnership ushers us into a creational project or to start up a community, where our relative reality can expand for the highest good of the many. Naturally, the partnerships can also be of a lesser fortunate character, being the adversaries of our past lives.

This work has to be engaged in as well to complete this cycle and eliminate all unfinished business. Whatever we encounter will be according to the content in our code sheets, the energy system and template. This includes present day tampering.

7. *The Correct Commitment is Key to Any Progress*
    This Principle governs the ambitions of what we commit to in life, energetically and physically. All we have learned from the previous Principles should at this point be a natural part of the energetic influential sphere the heart field produces, fueling our brain field to perceive the realities, we need to see to do our work. Based upon this information, using the Principles, the Rules and the Laws, the decisions can be made as in what to do, where to go and what to choose to go all-in to get the highest progression rate.

8. *The Correct Expression of Energy*
    When the Principles, the Rules and the Laws are an integrated part of our lives, and we live by them in thought, emotion and action, our world begins to change, because we have changed. The relative reality acts in our lives, with its feedback dynamics in whatever we experience, our daily energy work and in our self-observance. If we achieve the highest purity rate and the highest standards, we can reestablish a firm connection to the progressive grids, the holographic teaching system, as well as the ancient beneficial technologies to sustain and uphold our organic vessels.

At this point it is important to understand that the opposite version of the energy system can also become the end result of our clearing work, if the work with the Principles, the Rules and the Laws have been manipulated into an activation of hidden or inserted inverted genetics. This allows for the infected alter ego to enter into our energy system, take over the heart field and the brain field, and transform the remaining consciousness units into the inverted version.

The inverted genetics emit a type of cold light, and many have been tricked – in e.g. Kundalini activations – to think they have become enlightened and advanced humans, doing the greater good – notice this saying because that gives it away.

The inverted consciousness units are the complete opposite of the progressive consciousness units. Unfortunately, in present-day humans, it is possible to twist the Principles, the Rules and the Laws into producing a dark-light or crystalline-light energy system (the rainbow energy body). These energy bodies work as bridges into either the 3rd cycle or the reversed 5th cycle run by the inverted races.

Hence, everything we choose to engage in, in our inner work, has to be tested against if it has a progressive purpose and if it can apply to be of the highest good of the many. All has to be done with a highly attentive self-awareness along with taking responsibility for all our ego flaws, which are the access points into the 3rd cycle energies, and they are being used against us.

We have to keep asking, in all our choices: "What if everyone did this, how would the world look like?" and "How would I feel if this (which I am about to do now) was done to me?" The self-observance of the inner argumentation to do this or that, is key to avoid the twisted activation process.

9. *The Correct Expression of Power*

There is not much to say to this one, other than the activated heart field and brain field unfold the energies congruent with the activated consciousness units, and from that produce the progressive or the opposite energetic strength or power. The combined brain-heart influential sphere along with the double awareness will from this point interact with all surroundings, be it inner or outer, giving us the power to change things.

The inverted races are driven by an overly strong sense of self-righteousness and self-justification to do this or that, inclusive the lack of empathy and understanding of the consequences of the choices made. These traits in a human indicate a presence of inverted genetics in the template and energy system.

10. *The Correct Dignity*

Only if there is dignity in our original personality structure, can the progressive energies unfold into this vessel. The dignity drives us to, at all times, provide the most excellent results for the highest good of the many, for the reality and for all other lifeforms as well.

11. *The Correct Honor*

Honor was part of the ancient realities. It was developed in the 2nd evolutionary cycle, outside the pillar project, as we began the integration into the *manifested* planes of existence.

12. *The Correct Will*

Will was part of the ancient realities. It was developed in the 1st evolutionary cycle, outside the pillar project, as we began the integration into the *energetic* planes of existence.

On the 12 Rules of Engagement

The Rules of Engagement are not only aimed at how we behave and act around other people. They determine the energetic outcome of how we utilize the lifeforce and its counterpart within the racial grids.

Whenever we interact with any version of lifeforce, be it in a human, in another lifeform or whatever we are encountering, the Rules set the standards for the ways we should behave to keep the lifeforce pure in us, and in others.

The Rules, and how we utilize them to achieve the highest standards, determine the energetic result we attain in all our interactions, along with amplifying – or the opposite - the vibration energies in our heart field.

When we begin the work with progressive energy, new ways of how we behave are bound to come in play. Most of our human habits turn out to be counterproductive in our attempt to rebuild our energy system and they can be, to some degree, directly harmful.

Present-day humans have been turned into mindless consumers of all reality energies, which were meant to uphold our template and energy system, and turned into polluters of the lifeforce in the racial grids, which was meant to uphold our organic vessel and granting us life. Thus, part of the progression work is to learn how to multiply the resources of reality, sustain life and how to be around other humans and lifeforms by following the Rules. The processes to learn to utilize the Rules support the recreation of the lower order ego structure.

1. Correct Self-Mastery

We acknowledge that all is energy, and that energy is interconnected. We are lifeforms with different states of energy. Energy is utilized in our thoughts, our emotions and in the organic processes of the body. We affect other lifeforms with the energies we hold in the template, in the mind-field, the emotional field and the organic field. And lastly, these energies affect the racial grids, polluting the lifeforce. We must educate ourselves to again understand all energy, forces and powers.

2. Correct Self-Responsibility

In acknowledging, we affect everything by what we are energetically, be it humans, animals, plants and the world, we live in, we must take responsibility for our energetic state. We agree to take the energetic challenge of becoming harmless, which means not to directly harm, disrupt or digress whatever we interfere with. Unless, of course, the-whatever attacks us; then we are to defend ourselves appropriately.

In this, we accept that all disruptive belief systems and emotional patterns we might have, from this and previous lives, must be cleared and managed in the accurate ways, along with the distorted cellular construction, we call our body.

3. Correct Self-Expression

Following the understanding of the energetic consequences of how our ways and behavior affect other people, we must learn to express our ego, and its energetic emissions, in productive and amplificative ways for all implicated, leading to the highest good for all.

This means to energetically and genetically perceive, assess and recognize whatever is in front of us, and from this information act accordingly in ways, which will lead to the highest standards and the highest progression rate for all implicated. Here, naturally following the standards, ideas and ideologies of the progressive systems.

4. Correct Self-Containment

Following the first 3 Rules, we understand that we are responsible for not affecting others with the distorted energies and the genetics, we know, we hold in our template and energy system. We are to learn to contain these levels, until we have found ways to clear them.

Thus, we are observant of our behavior and energetic emissions around other lifeforms. We do whatever it takes, to ensure we do not give sustenance to the infected genetics and distorted energies in our energy system or template. We clear all that we can, all the time until we get it all. We make sure, we do not spread the infected genetics and energies into our surroundings. And we make sure, we do not set in motion the projective dynamics, amplifying the unwarranted levels in us and others. Even if this means going into isolation to attain the appropriate knowledge and gain the mastery of the infected energies, genetics and timelines involved.

Until we learn how to administer our own energies and genetics, it is prudent not to gather in teams or groups. Any group will amplify the unwarranted levels in all team members. At this time the focus must be on the individual activation and clearing work, and how to prepare for the NGC 2-8 racial segment activation. After the first phase, from 2026-2029, the community and team work can be reviewed.

5. Correct Team Awareness.
6. Correct Team Responsibility.
7. Correct Team Work in Projects.
8. Correct Progression Goals for the Project or Community, as a Team.
9. Correct Administration of all Inner Energies and Reality Resources.
10. Correct Management of all Outer Energies and Reality Resources.
11. Correct Deployment in Activity of Manifestation.
12. Correct Intentions of all Expected Outcome.

The 12 Choices of Living

When we begin the higher order progression work, there are many steps to take. One of them is the change of everything that runs our society. The 12 Choices of Living add to the Rules of Engagement and to the Principles to guarantee an equal progression possibility for all. The 12 choices also support our work to attain the highest purity rate, the highest standards and the highest progression rate.

1) We do not exploit other lifeforms to sustain our existence.
2) We do not exploit other lifeforms to support our progression.
3) We do not exploit other lifeforms to uphold or sustain our vessels.

4) We do not harness energy from others to build our energy system.
5) We do not take anything from others to support our progression.
6) We do not take anything from others to uphold our vessels.

7) We do not use the genetics from others to sustain our template.
8) We do not use the genetics from others to continue our race.
9) We do not use the genetics from others to develop or sustain our organic vessels.

10) We do not interfere with the realities of other lifeforms to sustain our existence.
11) We do not interfere with the realities of other lifeforms to do our progression.
12) We do not interfere with the realities belonging to other lifeforms to develop, uphold or sustain our organic vessels.

The 12 Natural Laws of Energy Utilization

The Natural Laws of Energy determine if the energies, we utilize in our energy system, will lead to progression or regression. When the energies are utilized correctly, we are allowed to reconnect to the reality holographic grids, and more energy will flow into our energy system via the base field and the organic holographic grid structure in the DE2. When utilized wrongly, the grids close down – step by step – until there is nothing left but regression and distortion.

1. The Law of Energetic Influence.

2. The Law of Proximity & Counterbalance.

3. The Law of Creational Projection and Amplification.

4. The Law of Correct Feedback and Reciprocity.

5. The Law of Higher and Lower Order Sciences.

6. The Law of the Cycles.

7. The Law of Cause and Effect.

8. The Law of Correct Function and Correct Use of Energy.

9. The Law of Correct Purpose and Correct Use of Genetics.

10. The Law of Correct Hierarchy and Emplacement.

11. The Law of Correct Use of Technology.

12. The Law of Continuation and Cyclic Renewal.

Meditate upon these Laws and write down what comes to mind.

For the 2nd Edition

On the Upgrade of the Universes

In 2007 the big withdrawal began. From that year, and onward, most of the factions, visitors, tourists and non-essential aliens began their departure from our system and returned to their own realities. Many other-dimensional humanoid races stayed behind, of course, having developed multiple businesses, planetoid realities and trade routes using our system as their hub, and just as many decided to take off, leaving behind their facilities, alien technologies and genetic projects.

Now, why this take off? In essence, because time was, and is, up. First and foremost, due to the ending of the timeline event, but also due to the fact that the numerous universes, bordering our universe, have reached their completion cycles and are, because of that, ready to elevate into new cycles. Most of the races are ready to move into the 5th cycle or the 7th cycle.

For some odd reason, not many of the races are going into the 6th cycle as if they deliberately choose to circumvent that one. And why is that? Well, perhaps it rests on the fact that the 6th cycle has to be unfolded within the progressive systems and realities, overseen by the human races. As part of the human races and in a human organic vessel (an original one, that is, not our current version of a human).[109]

If the regressed and humanoids had chosen the 6th cycle, they would not become part of the old pillar project, since that project did not complete its purpose in our sector, but become part of the progressive worlds that grew from the pillar project within other segments. The

---

[109] Think about it, these races have fought the human races for eons and now they have to become part of them? As a race. I tell you, most of the regressed would rather die a painful death and self-destruct than taking the 6th cycle as a human.

prolific pillar project races have constituted new evolutionary cycles and new versions of the human races in these sectors.

For that reason, it is equally important that the first ones that created the foundation of the 6th cycle are retracted from the regressed grids, realities and worlds, where they do not belong. If not as a free choice, given that it is impossible due to manipulation and exploitation, then as genetics and templates stored in the Library. This will happen when the Library is detached from the DE1 version of our system, during the 2-8 NGC activation and cleanup phase. If we cannot make the shift on our own, the original pillar genetics will be pulled out along with the Library. From here the genetics will be recalibrated and inserted into a fitting cycle within the future progressive worlds.

In contrast to the 6th cycle, the 5th cycle and the 7th cycle unfold within realities funded upon holographic-technological surroundings and a mixture of humanoid races, similar to most of the older versions of the humanoid and regressed worlds.[110]

And the humanoids prefer this version, because an upgrade into a higher cycle similar in energy and construction to the previous one, but on a higher dimensional level, allows for a complete transfer of the original code sheets, whereas a transfer into the human overseen evolutionary cycles, demands new code sheets, a different organic vessel and the genetic-energetic work with the unity consciousness. In many ways, a completely new beginning.

However, a version of the 6th evolutionary cycle has to be taken at some point, if any of these races want to move into the premium cycles, or the over-cycles, to call them by two new names. Unless, of

---

[110] Here a new distinction is to be observed. The regressed races are the original pillar project humans that succumbed to the timeline event, and the humanoid races are the original genetically different races from the universes outside the pillar project.

course, these races want to remain in the older universes, stuck in the old cycles, until they reach their devastation cycle and cease to exist.

The upgrading of the universes around us is therefore about the elevation of the cycles, once the old ones are done (or emptied out of energy and genetics), and it is time to move into the new cycles, get new organic vessels and start afresh within new reality fields. But, as we know, the humanoids and the regressed races are not really keen on that move, so chances are they will delay their forced elevation into the 6th cycle for as long as possible.

Nevertheless, for the time being, they have to return to their own realities to be able to do the lift into their chosen cycles, because an upgrade is only possible within their own racial grids. It is not possible to upgrade while being actively part of another universe. Hence, the return to their own homes. This return is expected to be completed in 2022.

Unsurprisingly, once they are done with the cyclic elevation, they will come back in their newly upgraded version and reconnect to their former projects here. This is a possibility, because the chance of our universe doing the uplifting, i.e. out of the holographic-technological reversed 5th cycle and back into the progressive 6th cycle, is slim. The many races, operating here, have ensured that the upgrading of our system will be directed into their reality settings by the engineering of the new earth project (crystalline-quantum based), overseen by the regressed races. The humanoid races from the adjacent universes can access that reality field as well. The new earth project is an artificial reality construction in the 5D somewhere around our planet and thus not the real 5D as part of the universal communities. It is still an enclosure, keeping humans exploited.

But of course, these races have not counted in the NGC in their devious plans. And that is precisely why the NGC was instigated to begin with and the pull out of the non-infected 6th pillar humans into other universes under the governance of the Ancient Ones. We knew this move would come from the regressed, at the end of the timeline event, where our system could reconnect to the progressive grids, and we prepared our countermove to ensure a wide-ranging return of the pillar project genetics to their own cycles.

Now, our system begins the infusions of the DE2 energies in 2022, but will remain under the control of the regressed races, unless of course the majority of humanity by some chance decides to wake up and return to what they are.

We kind of know how that one goes, so to end the tragedy of our system, the NGC plays a pivotal role as the freeing element, since few humans can do that on their own and thus need energetic assistance and a push in the right direction. At the same time, the NGC will release the original construction, behind our current system, from the regressed sector and ensure that the progressive racial grids, fused with the construction, can return to their appropriate segment within the progressive worlds. The future question is, whether the returning progressive holographic grids, racial grids and pillar project templates (the 6-12 pillar project templates) will remain as part of a rebooted and reset system, based upon its original code systems and replaced into the Sagittarius arm, or if it all will be pulled out and recreated in the progressive worlds as part of the Perseus arm in the 6th cycle.[111]

If the latter becomes the solution, to preserve and protect the construction, our work will be accordingly in the years to come.

However, if the solution becomes the shift into the Sagittarius arm, which is a mixed humanoid-human system connected to the universes outside the regressed systems, then our template work will reflect that. This book has mainly aimed at the Sagittarius solution. Only time can tell. We will know for sure around 2029.

---

[111] For those of you, who have missed that fact, our system was moved into the Orion arm in 2011 to connect us fully to the 3rd cycle energies and the machine worlds.

On the Changes in the Sun

In 2022 the sun will initiate its transformation into density 2 (DE2) to match the upgrading energies of the other universes around us, all of which will affect our solar system, and us, energetically. In 2007 the sun began the process of shedding off its density 1 (DE1) energies; in a way it has gone reverse since then, as it followed the various stages of the completion of the timeline event. The transition of the sun will be completed in 2021, in the northern hemisphere, and in 2022 in the southern.

Around the same time the NGC will hit the sun and our solar system as well. A month ago, it looked as it was only the NGC that would hit the sun in 2022, but now (March 2020) it is clear that it will be BOTH the upgrading energies of the other universes as well as the NGC.

Density 2 contains the sub-dimensions 4-6 (D4-D6), which are further divided into multiple minor reality fields. In DE2 the regressed worlds and progressive realities exist parallelly.

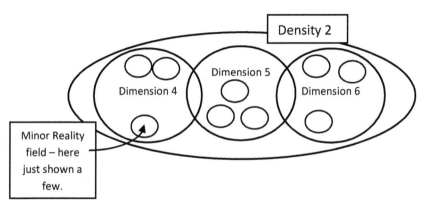

All viable universes with potentials for life, in our sector, will continue their evolutionary cycles within the DE2 as the lowest point of organic existence. And that is what is coming our way. Energetic upgrades on three fronts. That is bound to have a huge impact on the density 1.

Density 1 (our universe) holds the sub-dimensions of D1-D3. The DE1 is composed of timeline event energies in a mix of 3rd cycle and distorted D5 pillar energies from the Sirian system, infused with genetics from both.

The timeline event energies are decaying and most of the genetics from this period are now infested with the 3rd cycle energies. Because of the lack of energy, and the growing abyss beneath our universe, all that is within the DE1 must transform into the DE2 and what cannot, will be absorbed into the before the timeline event outdated 3rd cycle. This cycle was left behind eons ago and consequently it is not viable for a continuation of any prolonged organic existence. Only machines and crystalline races can exist there (which they already do).

As the sun shifts into the DE2, the energies will change profoundly. The shift of the sun could be likened with a letting go of an old energy body, and lifting up into a new. The DE2 level of the sun will detach from the DE1 level, leaving the shell behind in the DE1 section of our universe.

This means that the sun in the sky will be the dying DE1 version of our sun, and the DE2 version of our sun, in its higher energetic form, will continue its function within the continuing DE2 resonance fields. In essence, a transcension of the sun.

This process will have two main effects, all depending on which grids we are positioned on, i.e. following the relative reality dynamics.

The DE1 Scenario

For humans positioned within the DE1 frequency settings, the dying version of the sun will at first feel hotter and stronger, generating warmer weather. General science will not detect the stronger solar radiation as coming from the sun, but instead attribute it to a weaker magnetic field. Since the energies and life sustaining codes of the sun move into DE2, what remain in the DE1 will only be the outer kinetic processes of a dying star. Technically the sun has been in this process, for a long time, but the shift will increase the process.

However, since science has determined that our sun is viable for at least a million years or so, they will not see the changes in the sun (because they will not look for it) until the DE1 energies of the sun hit the spectrum of a white dwarf. Then, they will know, because the sun gets cooler and our planet will go into the long-prophesized ice age.

This stage of decay will be similar to what happened on the other DE1 planets in our solar system that completed this process ages ago. So, at first, humanity will experience a global warning, only to be followed by a global cooling. The timeframe of this is unknow. It will depend on the shift of intensity of the magnetic field.[112]

The DE2 Scenario

If we are following the NGC and the upgrading of our universe, the DE2 solar levels will fuel our lifeforce code sheets, as we similarly shift into a higher vibration. But only if we upgrade and work on our bio-field and energy system, following the stages of the NGC, and do the upgrading shifts of the universes around us. Both clusters of energies

---

[112] The magnetic field around our planet and the sun are interconnected. This is not a general scientific fact, because science assumes the magnetic field is generated by a molten core and the field around our planet is created by the kinetic effects of the rotation of the molten core. They assume that the energies of the sun are bounced off by the magnetic field, when they hit it, creating the aurora borealis.

will activate our hidden DE2 genetics – for good and ill – and our work will follow whatever shows up within our perception field from the chiasm (the pillar project template in us) as well as the genetics, we might have from outside the pillar project. Hence, the emplacement is meant to "shield" us from exposing this to other humans, as well as giving us the best conditions to work with what is coming on our own. As we know from the Rules of Engagement, the first rules teach us about self-containment and self-responsibility for what we are and that we are the ones to deal with it.

A positive side effect of following the NGC, is that the hotter DE1 sun will not affect us in the same manner as other people. We will adjust to the upgrading code sequences of the DE2 sun, along with the physical experiences of the sun. We will learn to have a "double sun exposure" on DE1 and DE2, and if we work with our bio-field to keep the organic cells at their highest purity rate, the warmth (aka its kinetic decay) of the sun will not be felt in the same way as others. We can adjust our bio-vessel to withstand the changes.

And, not to forget, we are to work against the decay and entropy rate of the DE1 organic cells, since the human bio-organic vessel will try to follow the decay rate of the sun. We are to work against this in our daily energy work, the way we live and the ways we conduct our energies. Difficult choices will have to be made. But that is for later.

The HAL Educations (2022-2025) work on the higher order sciences to meetup with the DE2 shift. The courses will outline the initial stages of the year-long work and then we educate ourselves to understand the organic vessel, amongst other important issues, in order to develop this as well all that we are as a human in the best ways.

The Three Levels of Energies

We have reached the middle section of the 3-9 pillar transformation process of the NGC, running from 2020-2022. The middle section of the NGC activates the code sheets and the holographic grids behind all energy systems, found in lifeforms and realities, on the radiation and vibration field levels. And that work coincides with the changes in the sun. Furthermore, the timeline event has reached its point zero state and that will affect the DE1 grids and old programs as well.

So, we have 3 factors in play, in our reality
1) The incoming NGC energies & the end of the timeline event.
2) The shift of the sun into DE2.
3) The upgrading of the universes around us.

This will make a nice recipe for energetic chaos to put it mildly. And this brew of energies will hit us on all 3 levels of our being, i.e. on the bio-field (following the NGC because of the holographic grid energies) on the emotional field (following the sun because of the vibration fields, in our energy system, connected to the sun) and on the mental field (following the completion of the timeline event, allowing the brain to shift back into the radiation field and thus open up for the universes "out there"). And not to forget the prohibiting technologies and the regressed genetics in our energy system, also affected by the 3-fold brew of energies.

However, the ways this unfold are different within the northern and southern hemispheres due to the differences in the grids running in these two parts of our world. The northern hemisphere is mainly operated via the 3-9 reality fields and 5-11 holographic-technological grids, and with that, the effects from the shift of the sun will be felt on a density 2, original dimension 3 (3rd cycle-D3) and D5 (regressive and progressive DE2-D5) level, similar to the dimensional settings we had in Atlantis. Plus, the northern grids are affiliated with the Atlantic and Arctic Ocean and the upper sections of the northern parts of the magnetic field.

Conversely, the southern hemisphere is mainly operated from a 4-10 systemic level, i.e. the interracial grids, seeding and operating in Australia as the base of global alien operations. Along with the well-hidden Lemurian versions of the 6-12 universal grids. Thus, the sun will affect the southern hemisphere on a density 2, original dimension 4 (regressive and progressive DE2-D4) and on a D6 level (regressive and progressive DE2-D6). The southern holographic reality grids are affiliated with Antarctica and the magnetic south pole.

The field lines of the magnetic field around our planet are different in composition, energetically speaking, and combined with the distinctly different sections of the holographic grids, north and south, the NGC incoming activation and cleanup energies will work differently on the grids in the two parts of our planet.

The holographic grids define the energetic settings on our planet on a DE2 level. In DE1, our current energetic setting, the energetic changes have not reached their full potentials, but as the DE2 from the sun and the incoming higher order energies of the NGC hit the core of our reality, in 2020-2022, these will affect the reality fields in a new way, compared to the activation and cleanup of the first 3 years of the NGC 3-9 phase, i.e. in 2017-2019. The next phase of the NGC energies will hit and amplify *the holographic grids* from 2020-2022. These grids are the ones that constitute our DE1 reality, and basically our world.

This is bound to generate effects in all lifeforms, as well as in nature, since all are built of holographic code systems, originally aligned with the resonance fields and the holographic grids of our reality. And yet, the differences will be dissimilar in the north and in the south.

The Effects

Aside from the "normal" human experience, the world has different grids operating on the DE2 levels of its original reality settings. The grids in the 6-12 pillar code settings, since our reality technically is a full 6-12 reality, only harbor the other lower grids due to transfer of the reality grids from the other pillars and their gone realities, today seen as the inner planets in our solar system, i.e. the regressed grids from the crystalline 3-9, fallen 4-10 and 5-11 regressed pillars.

Now, the regressed grids are operated by the intra-systemic races and their allied in the regressed and humanoid realities, and they are not eager to change their operations in our system. So, naturally all hands are on deck from their side to prevent the NGC from doing its work.

This counter-dynamic halt the incoming energies and generates wobbles in the reality grids. It can be compared to that of a flood that is being prevented from running its natural trajectory. To complete its course, the flood then finds other passages to run via. The NGC will do the same.

Two levels are affected by the NGC in the next 3 years – aside from the details provided so far in this book – the regressed genetics in humans and any other lifeform, as well as the holographic grids controlling the environment of the world. The holographic grids, the racial grids and their similar energies in the human energy system are the ones that will be targeted to prevent these from activating and clearing. Animals are targeted as well, since all lifeforms hold genetics that can be manipulated.

Since *the shields* that used to be above Australia are gone, the higher energies from Antarctica (the field lines are strongest around the poles, and the NGC will amplify the magnetic field, thus this will cause changes in the weather system of Antarctica) along with the sun amplifying the radiation level, as the field lines of Australia get amped up by the higher radiation level. This will set the new code standards for the world.

The Arctic will awaken as well. We have only seen the beginning of this, as the warmer water beneath the icecap will wear out the ice shelves and open up to the old grids, hidden beneath. As the upper level of the magnetic field sparks to life, the extremely ancient grids of the 6-12 pillar will activate as well. Lots will surface on the inner planes of perception as this happens. That will affect the racial grids and what the human genome can hold of energy.

North Magnetic Grid Activation: Racial grids following the awakening of the Arctic.

Southern Magnetic Grid Activation:
Holographic grids following with amplification of the Antarctica.

All factors are building up for more heat and more erratic weather worldwide as part of the terraforming of our planet, the genetic modification and the redistribution of wealth and power, but mostly seen in Australia where all things will manifest first. But humans can adapt to the higher radiation level, if they live in a higher energetic state, following the highest purity rate (turning herbivore or frugivore is the first step). And if they do the needed energy work to clear and follow the 3-fold energy combination of changes. So, for now, enough information has been given. Go to my website to get access to all the free material, do the classes and stay tuned for what is coming.

The areas of change that have to be done, to adapt into a DE2 personality structure and DE2 organic vessel.

Printed in Australia
AUHW011954280520
328442AU00025B/466

9 788743 015451